LOWCARB**CHINESE**COOKING

CHARMAINE
SOLOMON

LOWCARB**CHINESE**COOKING

NEW
HOLLAND

Published in Australia in 2005 by New Holland Publishers (Australia) Pty Ltd
Sydney • Auckland • London • Cape Town

14 Aquatic Drive Frenchs Forest NSW 2086 Australia
218 Lake Road Northcote Auckland New Zealand
86 Edgware Road London W2 2EA United Kingdom
80 McKenzie Street Cape Town 8001 South Africa

First edition published in 1979 by Summit Books, Paul Hamlyn Pty Limited
This edition published in 2005 by New Holland Publishers (Australia) Pty Ltd

National Library of Australia Cataloguing-in-Publication Data:

Solomon, Charmaine.
       Low Carb Chinese Cooking

       Includes index.
       ISBN .1 74110 316 9.

       1. Cookery, Chinese. 2. Low-carbohydrate diet—Recipes. I. Title.

       641.5951

Publishing Manager: Fiona Schultz
Project Editor: Lliane Clarke
Designer: Joanne Buckley

Printer: SNP Leefung Printers, China

10 9 8 7 6 5 4 3 2

Front cover images: Stir Fried Prawns in the Shell (page 64) top, Mongolian Lamb (page 123) bottom.
Back cover images: Clockwise from top left: Garlic Scallops (page 66), Hors d'Oeuvres (page 25), Stuffed Bitter Melon in
Black Bean Sauce (page 149), Steamed Fish Balls with Snow Peas (page 41).

Preface

There are some people without whom this book would not have happened. It started with my husband Reuben.

Some years ago a doctor told Reuben to lose weight and limit the carbohydrates in his diet because a blood test showed a triglyceride count that was higher than it should be. Talking with the physician about which foods my husband was allowed, I realised it would be hard to confine a dedicated Asian food freak to steaks, salads, steamed fish and chicken, so I had to use the foods that were permitted, in a way that would keep him happy. The answer? Chinese food.

There had to be modifications, of course. No unlimited portions of rice because this doesn't fit in with a low carbohydrate diet. Measured quantities are allowed, and set off the main dishes featuring fish, poultry, lean meat and low carbohydrate vegetables. Cholesterol was not a problem so there was no bar to fried dishes, but I sensibly kept the amount of oil to a minimum and used the stir-frying method.

In the space of six weeks the scales showed a loss of 6.3 kg and friends commented on his new, trim shape. The next blood analysis revealed that triglyceride levels had dropped right back to within normal range.

Shortly after, while I was a guest on a popular radio show, the co-host of the show was being teased about his increasing girth. I remarked that being a lover of Chinese food he could lose weight easily and enjoy the process if he chose the right kind of Chinese food. The station switchboard lit up as people wanted to know more about how this could be achieved.

There was no going back! I talked my publisher into letting me do this book, giving it priority over another I was working on.

May every reader who decides to give it a trial be as appreciative as the physician from the UK who contacted me to say he had great success losing weight and lowering his triglycerides using these receipes.

I also acknowledge all the nutritionists, dietitians and diet gurus who challenged the belief that calorie/kilojoule counting was the only way to lose weight and gave millions of people a choice....The Quick Weight Loss Diet, the Zone Diet, the Fit for Life Diet, the South Beach Diet and others too numerous to mention. This just happens to be the one that worked for us.

Acknowledgments

Without the dedication of my daughters Nina and Deborah, and the painstaking
care of photographer David Marshall, there would be no way to convey
to the readers of this book how tempting these recipes are.

Nina is one of the most accurate food stylists I have seen in action. I thought I was particular,
because when I cooked food for my earlier books I insisted on including every seasoning that
was called for … even salt. It wasn't going to show, but I wanted the food to be eaten and
enjoyed, not wasted, after it had finished posing for the camera. This must have rubbed off
on Nina, because the food she prepared for the camera tasted just the way it should.

Deborah, a trained food person, was a great assistant, offering her cooking expertise and
her lovely home and courtyard for the seafood shots. Penny Crino, Nina's long time friend,
was a cheerful and meticulous kitchen hand whose support was much appreciated by Nina.

I am grateful to these young women, all of whom have full and busy lives,
for putting other matters on hold to create these tempting pictures.

I would also like to thank the Australian Government Publishing Service
for allowing me to compile the carbohydrate values of Western foods
from the Tables of Composition of Australian Foods,

Contents

Introduction ■■□

Losing weight on a Chinese diet is easy and it's fun. You should never feel hungry or deprived while using these recipes, because every meal will be as exciting visually and taste-wise as a meal at a first-class Chinese restaurant.

No, this is not impossible. Here's how it works. The recipes I have chosen suit a low carbohydrate diet. But they differ from other low carbohydrate diet recipes because they are also low fat recipes. This makes them, in line with modern nutritional thinking, healthier.

How the diet works

Why a low carbohydrate diet rather than a kilojoule controlled diet? Mainly because with counting energy units, which is all kilojoules are, the results are very slow. As every dieter knows, this is discouraging and gives no incentive to stay with the diet. Also, you feel hungry much of the time.

On a low carbohydrate intake the weight comes off much faster, and because of the variety and quantity of protein foods permitted you do not feel hungry. If you feel the portions are too small eat more meat, poultry or seafood. But don't eat more than the stated amounts of vegetables or rice—that is where the carbohydrates lurk for the unwary.

There's nothing new or startling about losing weight on a low carbohydrate diet. Doctors and nutritionists have been telling us about the effectiveness of cutting carbohydrates rather than calories for some time now.

What is new is that here is a way to adapt delicious, flavoursome Chinese food to a low carbohydrate diet. This book enables you to count the amount of carbohydrates in each recipe so that you can calculate your daily intake.

There are no set menus. Knowing the carbohydrate count of each dish, you can make a wise choice to suit the occasion and keep losing weight while enjoying your favourite kind of food.

In this very flexible eating program you are not urged to have a hearty breakfast—so many people are just not hungry early in the morning. But breakfast should not be a problem even if you are a big breakfast eater. Eggs, bacon, grilled ham and omelettes are sustaining high protein foods with hardly a gram of carbohydrate between them. Limited to one slice of toast, the only real carbohydrate in such a meal would be in the toast—approximately 11 or 12 grams to a small slice. Unsweetened tea or coffee (or artificially sweetened) is permitted, but be wary of fruit juices because they have a high carbohydrate content.

Lunch need not be boring, either. You are not told that on Mondays you should lunch on cottage cheese and on Tuesday hard boiled eggs or tuna. What you choose is up to you, as long as you eat foods that are not loaded with carbohydrates. If you are at home and can cook yourself a light lunch, eat two Chinese meals a day and keep on losing weight. If you carry your lunch to work, cold Red Cooked Chicken or Smoked Tangerine Chicken would be ideal.

If you lunch at a restaurant choose fish, meat or chicken prepared in a way that does not include a starchy coating (such as batter or breadcrumbs) or a thickened sauce. For instance, seafood cocktail followed by steak or roast chicken served with a tossed salad or a green vegetable would be ideal. You would take in very little carbohydrate with such a choice. But if you were to have crumbed fish or battered prawns served with potato chips, or poultry or meat in a sauce thickened with flour and served with a bread roll, you could reach almost your entire daily quota of carbohydrate.

Avoid the pitfalls mentioned here and you will have enough points left out of your daily total to enjoy a very good evening meal such as Beef in Black Bean Sauce (7 grams per portion) or Braised Ginger Chicken (6 grams). Even if you had rice with it (half a cup of cooked rice contains 18 carbohydrate grams), you'd still be within your allowance.

Beside each recipe you will find a table giving the carbohydrate content of each ingredient and the total amount for the recipe. Where you see the letters Tr (trace) the amount of carbohydrate is 0.5 grams, or less. I have given Tr a value of 0.5 grams to make the additions simpler.

To help you make up your own eating program there are two tables of carbohydrate values at the back of this book, beginning on page 184. One gives the figures for the Chinese ingredients used in the recipes. The other gives the figures for Western foods, so you can make up alternative meals and still follow your low carbohydrate diet. Study the tables. Get used to the fact that a steak or a lamb chop contains no carbohydrates but two sandwiches, each using two slices of bread, will chalk up between 46 and 58 grams of carbohydrate (depending on the type of bread used), more than half your daily allowance! A doughnut will cost you 18 to 20 grams of carbohydrate; a slice of cream sponge with icing, 24 grams; and a wedge of apple pie, 52.6 grams.

You should also be wary of some fruits, although you may enjoy others with impunity. Cantaloupe, or rockmelon, is among the lowest in carbohydrate—half a cantaloupe 10 cm (4 in) in diameter contains less than 7 grams. Two small or one large mandarin contains 11.2 grams and even avocados, notoriously banned from low calorie diets, are okay—less than 7 grams in half a medium avocado. A medium banana has 22.5 grams of carbohydrate and a medium pear 20.8 grams. Detailed carbohydrate tables are available at most pharmacies or drug stores if you want to know about other foods that are not covered in this book.

A certain number of grams of carbohydrate are permitted—indeed necessary—but this figure varies with each individual and the amount of regular physical activity.

Before you start on any reducing diet you should ask your doctor to recommend how much weight you should lose and how quickly you should lose it. Many physicians are against rapid weight loss, while others feel the end justifies the means when excessive weight is endangering health.

The intake of carbohydrate considered necessary for good health varies considerably, even on a weight loss diet, but 80 grams of carbohydrate a day is a safe amount by the standards of most nutritionists. For faster weight loss the intake could be reduced to 60 grams a day, but only with the approval of your doctor. On this daily intake of carbohydrate, and while living a moderately active life, there should be a regular weight loss of at least 2 kilogrammes (4.5 lbs) a week, which will level off as you reach your ideal weight.

If, on a daily allowance of 80 grams carbohydrate, you are not losing weight fast enough, it could be that you're a very slow burner and need to add a 30 minute brisk walk to the daily routine On the other hand, if you're a fast burner you may be able to add a few more grams of carbohydrate and still lose weight at a rate that makes you feel you're gaining your goal. It is largely a matter of metabolism—and, of course, not cheating!

As excess kilos come off and you reach your ideal weight, start adding more carbohydrates to stabilise at the weight you want to be. Don't add them in the form of white sugar and candies. Instead, try whole cereals, raw or lightly cooked vegetables and fresh fruit, which also give you vitamins and essential fibre. Make those portions a little more generous. Find out for yourself just what your metabolism can handle to keep your weight stable while allowing you to enjoy your favourite foods for the rest of a long and healthy life.

Fats and starches

On a diet that counts carbohydrates rather than calories you don't have to remove the skin from chicken and you can use fatty pork, unlike some diets which call for every bit of fat to be trimmed off. But even the strongest digestion can't take a lot of fat without having a large amount of starch food to absorb the richness, so keep fats to a minimum and have a greater feeling of well being.

One of the good things about the recipes in this book is that you feel well fed without feeling you have over-eaten. Giving preference to the steamed and stir-fried dishes is sensible, but you can add touches such as fried almonds (not too many) and know that even if you crunch on a dozen or so with your Chicken and Almonds the total carbohydrate count is still well under the score for a handful of potato chips.

You will not find any thick, gluey sauces in these recipes. Such sauces are associated with cheap Chinese take-away food. Good, classic Chinese cooking usually has just enough sauce to flavour the main ingredients. Where I have included a sauce I have allowed only enough thickening to provide some body, or I have deleted the thickening altogether.

Steer clear of sweet and sour sauces with their high proportion of sugar and cornflour. You won't find any in this book, but remember this when eating out.

You will not miss the heavy sauces after a few days. Your taste buds will have responded to the natural juices of the ingredients, with their subtle or robust flavours, and you may not want to thicken a sauce ever again!

I would like to recommend that you use natural brown rice, although it's not usually served with Chinese meals. If brown rice doesn't appeal to you, try a mixture of brown and white rice. Brown rice has a much firmer texture, takes longer to chew and is more satisfying than white rice. Brown rice is also better for you nutritionally. But remember, there are about 18 grams of carbohydrate in half a cup of cooked rice of any kind, white or brown. Depending on how many grams of carbohydrate you had at other meals, you may be able to managed ½ cup of cooked rice or noodles with your main dish. Try to keep the daily total at 80 grams (or 60 grams if a quicker weight loss in demanded by your physician.)

Using oils

Most doctors will approve a low carbohydrate, low fat diet (such as this one) provided it is well balanced. Your doctor, who has your health record readily available, can tell you what other factors must be considered.

If your physician recommends that you should use only polyunsaturated fats, substitute sunflower or maize oil for peanut oil. Safflower oil is highest in polyunsaturates, but when heated it sometimes has a strong odour that could affect the flavour of dishes cooked in it. Sunflower and maize oils have a neutral odour.

There are a few recipes which call for deep frying. If the oil is hot enough to seal the food and if you don't fry too much at once (which lowers the temperature and allows the food to absorb the oil) there will be no excessive greasiness, just the flavour and moisture sealed in. Drain the cooked food well on absorbent paper.

Flavourings

An added bonus when dieting on Chinese food is that you are not deprived of interesting flavours. Garlic and ginger, soy sauce, sesame oil, five spice powder, the basic flavourings that give Chinese food its character, are permissible. I have used sauces that are low in carbohydrates and avoided such sweet sauces as plum and barbecue sauce.

The hot, Sichuan style dishes add interest and pungent flavours. Chilli bean sauce and soy chilli sauce are excellent additions to your range of seasonings, but use them with caution because they are very hot!

The clear, well-flavoured soups in this collection of recipes are filling and good for you. Add pieces of chicken, seafood or red meat, or stir a beaten egg into the simmering soup.

Beverages

Chinese tea is the best thing to drink with Chinese meals. It gives you a feeling of well-being, seeming to aid digestion and prevent that bloated feeling. The Chinese believe it is a very healthy drink and helps to offset the richness of the meal.

Forget the usual rules for making tea. One teaspoon of Chinese tea leaves will be enough for three or four cups of boiling water, which will fill quite a few of those tiny Chinese tea cups. You can add more boiling water to the pot as the brew strengthens, but remember—Chinese tea is never served with milk or sugar. There are various types to try, too, such as polee, oolong, jasmin and lychee.

If you are a dedicated wine drinker it will please you to know you can drink a glass or two of dry wine (white wine is best with Chinese food) without ruining your diet. You may even have a nip of whisky, brandy or other spirits before your meal. Beer, sweet sherry, sweet vermouth and liqueurs are high in carbohydrates, so avoid them.

Servings

Many of the recipes are in two-portion quantities because there are probably two people in the family who want to lose weight. If others want to join the Chinese dieting program the recipes can be doubled easily. Those who don't need to lose weight will enjoy the dishes too, with as much extra rice or noodles as they wish.

The recipes are also designed as a main dish for two people, or four people if a second dish is served.

Soups have been given in four-portion amounts because it takes time to prepare the stock and it hardly seems worthwhile just making enough for two. Extra stock can be frozen and soups can be refrigerated and reheated. If you're reheating a soup, add a fresh sprinkle of chopped spring onions or fresh coriander before serving to make the flavour even better.

Please don't attempt to double any stir-fried recipe designed for four people because the stir-frying technique is not suitable for cooking more than 500 g (1 lb) of meat, seafood or poultry at one time. You'll get much better results if you prepare two lots of ingredients and cook them separately—and the extra cooking time is only a few minutes.

Choosing the right menu

Remember that any dieting program will only work as well as you let it. The dishes have been carefully trimmed of excess carbohydrates, but it's up to you to select carefully so that you don't exceed your daily allowance of carbohydrate grams.

Many of the recipes are so low in carbohydrates that you could have a dish of prawns and another of beef at the same meal.

Entertaining guests

Some of the most luxurious and tasty Chinese dishes are surprisingly low in carbohydrates, so if you're entertaining and want to show off without blowing your diet sky-high, you can do so. The richer and more luxurious recipes have been scaled for four or more servings. If you control the amount of rice or noodles you eat with these dishes, your guests will never know you're losing weight as you sit down and enjoy a delicious meal with them.

I have cheated a little by drastically cutting the amount of almonds or water chestnuts used in some recipes but have included enough to provide taste and texture without upsetting your diet.

Enjoying your food

I have tried to satisfy the gourmet that lurks inside every would-be dieter, and as you try some of the more unusual ingredients you will discover new tastes and textures to make mealtimes more interesting.

You can enjoy wonderful flavours and exotic dishes, but they are almost totally free of fattening ingredients. Lean meats, poultry, seafood and selected vegetables have been used. Recipes have been trimmed of ingredients that would prove detrimental by upsetting the carbohydrate balance. Thick sauces have been eliminated. This book gives you meals you will enjoy eating even when you are down to your desired weight.

The pleasure of cooking

One of the most frustrating things about being on a diet is not just cutting down on eating, but cutting down on the creative part—cooking. For anyone who likes to cook, this deprives them of two satisfactions.

The techniques of cutting, shredding, chopping and marinating, the split second timing of stir-frying, and the visual and taste appeal of the low carbohydrate dishes in this book should take care of all the yearnings of the keen home cook. If you are already familiar with Chinese cooking you will use the knowledge you have. If it is new to you it will be fun learning to master the fine slicing, shredding and roll-cutting that are part of the art.

You will find that these meals are surprisingly economical. A quantity of steak that would feed two people in a Western style steak meal will feed four or even six when treated the Chinese way.

A variety of tastes

Another good thing about this eating plan is that you're still creating delicious, flavoursome food with lots of visual appeal. There is the fun of going marketing, choosing the smoothest, reddest capsicums, the crispest celery, finding Chinese vegetables you haven't tried before and discovering fascinating ingredients that may have been unknown to you. Ingredients like star anise, a beautifully shaped seed pod used for flavouring; lily buds, also called 'golden needles'; dried Chinese shitake mushrooms, full of inimitable flavour; bean sauces of different kinds to add excitement and extra protein; straw mushrooms with their intriguing structure (the miniature mushroom grows within an enveloping capsule), dried wood fungus, which has no flavour but adds texture; peeled walnuts, which don't become bitter when cooked; fresh bean sprouts, nature's powerhouse of vitamins; snow peas, once a rarity and still quite expensive, but just a few add a touch of sweetness and crisp texture.

Tricks that help

- Using a small plate or bowl makes portions look larger. Buy some Chinese rice bowls 10 cm (4 in) in diameter. These are the size used in restaurants and are a good size for both soups and solid foods.
- Eat with chopsticks. It is a skill easily learned—and if it slows you down, all the better. Your meals will take longer to eat and you will feel well fed. Eating fast often means eating more than you really need. Eating slowly and taking notice of what you eat will reduce food intake and increase enjoyment.
- If you are having more than one dish, bring each one to the table on its own and allow little pauses between courses. A bowl of soup to start the meal, followed by a dish of meat or fish combined with vegetables and cups of light, fragrant Chinese tea makes an enjoyable meal while working towards your ideal weight.
- Don't cook more of anything than you need for one meal. It is always a temptation to finish it rather than waste it.
- If you don't own a wok, invest a few dollars and buy one. It is definitely the best utensil for cooking Chinese food and because of its shape very little oil is needed, which keeps the fat content of these dishes low. You will find an explanation of the wok cooking technique on page 16.
- I hope this program becomes not just a one-time thing but a way of eating to keep you feeling fit and looking fabulous.

Utensils for Chinese cooking ■ ■ ■

Almost every Chinese dish can be prepared in a Western kitchen using Western equipment. But if you are keen on cooking Chinese food and want to buy special utensils, here is a guide to the most useful.

The wok

If you want to cook Chinese style, I would urge you to buy a wok before you even start to cook your first Chinese meal because it makes everything so much easier. It is truly an all-purpose cooking utensil. In it you boil, braise, fry and steam. While you can do all these things in pans you already possess, the wok is almost indispensable for the stir-frying technique that many Chinese dishes call for.

You may, of course, use a large, deep frying pan, but I have cooked stir-fried dishes in a deep frying pan, side by side with a wok, and I say without hesitation that the wok's a winner every time. Because of its spherical shape and high, flaring sides you can toss with abandon and stir-fry ingredients without their leaping over the sides. Because it is made of thin iron you get the quick, high heat so necessary in Chinese cooking. With a wok you can do everything the recipes in this book require and achieve the best results.

Don't feel you've got to pay a lot and buy a stainless steel or other expensive wok. Modestly priced iron woks are the best. They heat up more quickly and evenly, and if you remember to dry them well after washing, they will not rust. The handles get rather hot, but I've found that winding two or three layers of insulating tape around them keeps the handles quite comfortable to hold. The 35 cm (14 in) wok is the most useful.

To season your wok

An iron wok must be prepared before it is used by washing thoroughly with hot water and detergent. Some woks, when new, have a lacquer-like coating and this must be removed by almost filling the wok with water, adding about 2 tablespoons of bicarbonate of soda, and boiling for about 15 minutes. This softens the coating and it may be scrubbed off with a fine scourer. If some of the coating still remains, repeat the process until the wok is free from any coating on the inside. Dry well, place over gentle heat, then wipe over the entire inside surface with a wad of paper towel dipped in peanut oil. Repeat with more oil-soaked paper until the paper remains clean. Allow to cool. Your wok is now ready for use.

After use, do not scrub the wok with steel wool or abrasives. Soak to soften any remaining food, rub gently with a sponge or dish mop, using hot water and detergent. This preserves the surface. And make sure the wok is quite dry because if moisture is left in the pan it will rust. A well-used wok will soon turn black, but this is normal. And the more a wok is used, the better it is to cook in.

Chinese chopper

The Chinese chopper or cleaver may look clumsy to the uninitiated, but is the best thing for slicing, shredding, chopping and dicing. As an extra bonus, its wide blade, about 9 cm (3½ in) across and twice that in length can be used to transport cut up ingredients from chopping block to cooking pan. Use it on a wooden block or board. I do not recommend laminated chopping boards, whatever kind of knife you use. Young homemakers often succumb to their attractive appearance, but when you get down to serious cooking there's nothing to take the place of a solid wooden chopping block.

Steamers

The Chinese use steamers of aluminium or bamboo, but these are not essential. Steaming may be done in any covered pot large enough to accommodate a plate placed on a rack or a bowl to hold it well above the level of the water. The plate should be of a size that will allow free circulation of steam around and above it. The food to be cooked is placed on the plate, the pot covered with a well-fitting lid, and there you have a perfectly adequate improvised steamer.

Other kitchen aids

Chinese ladles, frying spoons and long bamboo chopsticks are useful, but not strictly necessary if you have other utensils that will do the job. Any kind of ladle may be used for dipping out stock and I have found that the curved, slotted spatula available so cheaply from chain stores or hardware departments is ideal for tossing and stir-frying. It is supposed to crush, strain, whip and lift and, if the makers only knew, is ideal for stir-frying as well.

For deep frying, the Chinese wire frying spoons are useful. A medium to large spoon can cope with a whole fish, lifting it out of the oil with ease, which is a consideration if you like deep fried whole fish.

Long wooden cooking chopsticks are also useful, especially for separating noodles as they cook, and for a variety of other jobs too.

Wok technique

Using a wok is not difficult. Just make sure the wok sits steadily on the stove, with no danger of tipping over. You can buy a large metal ring that serves as a secure base for the wok.

Make sure the heat is carefully controlled when simmering or braising. Being of thin metal, cooking takes place more quickly than in conventional utensils, so stir from time to time and ensure there is enough liquid to prevent burning. A little concentration the first few times will help you appreciate the shorter cooking time and when you get used to it you may find yourself becoming impatient with conventional cooking pans.

Stir-frying is the only wok cooking technique which is different from methods used in Western cooking. This is the method used for those short-cooked Oriental dishes that appear as if by magic at the roadside food stalls of Asian cities. If you have not been to Asia, and seen the method being used, then stir-frying might need some explanation. The 'stir' in stir-frying is not the same slow circular motion used in Western cookery, it is something more spectacular and unrestrained. It involves tossing, flipping, turning over, everything kept moving at speed so that all the surfaces of the food come into contact with the hot sides of the wok and the thin coating of oil.

The essence of stir-frying is split second timing, so when making a stir-fried dish every bit of preparation must be completed before cooking starts. The ingredients must be sliced, diced, marinated or whatever the recipe calls for. The seasonings should be measured out and placed in a handy position.

Don't be tempted to double quantities when stir-frying—the smaller the amount cooked at a time, the better the result. Certainly no more than 500 g (1 lb) should go into the wok at once because the temperature will drop, the meat will stew rather than fry, and the result will be disappointing.

Read the recipe carefully and arrange everything in the order in which it will be required. Once you start to cook there's no stopping to find a dash of this or that—you will interrupt the rhythm of the cooking. Ingredients are added in a pre-arranged order, those which take longest to cook going into the wok first and others following at intervals so that they are all cooked at the same time. It may seem difficult if you haven't tried it, but study a recipe first and you will see how logical it is.

Once you have cooked a stir-fried dish (after properly organising the ingredients) you will become addicted, as I have, to this method of cooking. It's so wonderfully quick and the results are delicious.

Remember to heat the wok before adding the oil. Pick up the wok by the handles and swirl to coat the sides with the oil before adding any ingredients. Since so little oil is used in stir-frying, swirling ensures it is spread over the inner surface so ingredients will not stick.

Stir-fried dishes must be served immediately they are ready or they will continue to cook in their own heat, losing the crisp texture and special flavour that comes from the fierce heat and short cooking time. So before you start to cook have the serving plate heated and ready, guests hungry and waiting, and let no time be lost in serving. Bon appetit!

Guide to weights and measures

The metric weights and metric fluid measures used in this book are those of the Standards Association of Australia. A good set of scales, a graduated Australian Standard measuring cup and a set of measuring spoons will be very helpful and can be obtained from leading hardware and kitchenware stores.

All cup and spoon measurements are level:

- The Australian Standard measuring cup has a capacity of 250 millilitres (250 ml).
- The Australian Standard tablespoon has a capacity of 20 millilitres (20 ml).
- The Australian Standard teaspoon has a capacity of 5 millilitres (5 ml).

In all recipes, imperial equivalents of metric measures are shown in parentheses, e.g. 500 g (1 lb) beef. Although the metric yields of cup and weighed measures are approximately 10 per cent greater than the imperial yields, the proportions remain the same. Therefore, for successful cooking use either metric or imperial weights and measures—do not mix the two.

New Zealand, British, United States and Canadian weights and measures are the same as Australian weights and measures except that:

(a) the Australian and British Standard tablespoons have a capacity of 20 millilitres (20 ml) whereas the New Zealand, United States and Canadian Standard tablespoons have a capacity of 15 millilitres (15 ml), therefore all tablespoon measures should be taken generously in those countries;

(b) the imperial pint (Australia, New Zealand and Britain) has a capacity of 20 fl oz whereas the pint used in the United States and Canada has a capacity of 16 fl oz, therefore pint measures should be increased accordingly in those two countries.

The following charts of conversion equivalents will be useful:

Oven temperature guide

The Celsius and Fahrenheit temperatures in the chart below relate to most gas ovens. Increase by 20°C or 50°F for electric ovens or refer to the manufacturer's temperature guide. For temperatures below 160°C (325°F), do not increase the given temperature.

Description of oven	Celsius °C	Fahrenheit °F	Gas Mark
Cool	100	200	¼
Very Slow	120	250	½
Slow	150	300	2
Moderately Slow	160	325	3
Moderate	180	350	4
Moderately Hot	190	375	5
Hot	200	400	6
Very Hot	230	450	8

Imperial Weight	Metric Weight
½ oz	15 g
1 oz	30 g
2 oz	60 g
3 oz	90 g
4 oz (¼ lb)	125 g
6 oz	185 g
8 oz (½ lb)	250 g
12 oz (¾ lb)	375 g
16 oz (1 lb)	500 g
24 oz (1½ lb)	750 g
32 oz (2 lb)	1000 g (1 kg)
3 lb	1500 g (1.5 kg)
4 lb	2000 g (2 kg)

Key: oz = ounce; lb = pound; g = gram; kg = kilogram.

Imperial Liquid Measures	Cup Measures	Metric Liquid Measures
1 fl oz		30 ml
2 fl oz	¼ cup	
3 fl oz		100 ml
4 fl oz (¼ pint US)	½ cup	
5 fl oz (¼ pint imp.)		150 ml
6 fl oz	¾ cup	
8 fl oz (½ pint US)	1 cup	250 ml
10 fl oz (½ pint imp.)	1¼ cups	
12 fl oz	1½ cups	
14 fl oz	1¾ cups	
16 fl oz (1 pint US)	2 cups	500 ml
20 fl oz (1 pint imp.)	2½ cups	

Key: fl oz = fluid ounce; ml = millilitre.

Appetisers

Starting the meal with a little something to take the edge off your hunger while satisfying the taste buds is a good idea on any diet. All the recipes in this section are based on high protein food which will do just that.

Many of these recipes are good for parties because they can be prepared beforehand and make interesting nibbles during the pre-dinner period.

The cold chicken dishes, steamed mushrooms and egg roll are also good to keep in mind when you have to carry a lunch to work and realise that a sandwich will cost you at least 24 grams of carbohydrate, almost a third of your daily ration. Pack a dainty selection of cold meats (Red Cooked Chicken is particularly suitable) or the appetisers mentioned above, but allow yourself more than an appetiser portion. Even if you were to eat half of the Egg Roll recipe (which serves 8 as an hors-d'oeuvre) you would still be under 6 grams of carbohydrate, and that's pretty good for a sustaining lunch.

Lettuce Rolls with Pork and Prawns

0	2 tablespoons peanut oil
5	2 tablespoons pine nuts
1	1 teaspoon crushed garlic
1	1 teaspoon finely grated fresh ginger
0	250 g (8 oz) minced pork
0	2 tablespoons hot water
2	125 g (4 oz) raw prawns, finely chopped
2	2 teaspoons bean sauce (mor sze jeung)
1	2 teaspoons oyster sauce
2	1 teaspoon hoi sin sauce
1	1 teaspoon red bean curd
4	1 teaspoon white sugar
2.5	¼ cup chopped bamboo shoot
2	1 spring onion, finely chopped
2.5	1 teaspoon cornflour (cornstarch)
0	1 tablespoon cold water
3.6	12 lettuce cups
29.6	**total grams carbohydrate**

In this modified recipe for Sahng Choy Bao, a favourite Chinese entree, each lettuce roll totals a mere 2.5 carbohydrate grams. Recipes like this prove that you can enjoy delicious food on a weight loss diet.

Heat peanut oil in a wok and on gentle heat fry the pine nuts until golden. Lift out on slotted spoon and drain on absorbent paper. Raise heat and when wok and oil are very hot add the garlic and ginger, stir quickly and almost immediately add the pork. Stir-fry until the pork has lost every trace of pinkness. Add the hot water, cover and cook for a few minutes so that pork is well done.

When liquid has evaporated add the prawns and stir-fry for 1 minute, mix together all the sauces, bean curd and sugar then add to wok. Stir and cook for 1 minute, mixing the seasonings well through the pork and prawns. Add bamboo shoot and spring onion and stir until heated through. Push ingredients to side of wok and thicken any remaining liquid with the cornflour mixed smoothly with cold water, allowing it to boil for 1 minute. Remove from heat and mix the pine nuts through. Serve the savoury mixture in a bowl, accompanied by crisp lettuce cups on a separate platter.

The rolls are meant to be assembled and eaten using the fingers. Put a spoonful of filling in one of the lettuce cups, roll up and eat it rather like a spring roll without pastry.

Lettuce Rolls with Pork and Prawns

Steamed Stuffed Mushrooms

Serves: 4–6

8	250 g (8 oz) fresh button mushrooms
4	250 g (8 oz) prawns
14.2	6 water chestnuts, finely chopped
Tr	1 egg white, slightly beaten
2	1 tablespoon light soy sauce
0	¾ teaspoon salt
Tr	½ teaspoon finely grated fresh ginger
2	½ teaspoon sugar
0	sesame oil
Tr	fresh coriander (cilantro) leaves to garnish
31.7	**total grams carbohydrate**

Choose mushrooms of an even size, about 4 cm (1½ in) across. Wipe mushrooms with a damp paper towel. Do not peel. Remove stems carefully with a little twist, leaving caps intact. Reserve stems for another use.

Shell, de-vein and finely chop prawns. Put prawns, water chestnuts, egg white and all seasoning ingredients into a bowl and mix thoroughly. Put a teaspoonful of the mixture into each mushroom cap, mounding it very slightly and firming the filling into the cap. Put in a heatproof dish lightly coated with sesame oil, cover dish tightly with foil, and steam mushrooms for 25–30 minutes. Allow to cool slightly and serve garnished with a few sprigs of fresh coriander leaves, if desired.

If mushrooms are being served as appetisers, save liquid in dish for adding to soups or sauces. If they are part of a meal, thicken liquid slightly by bringing to the boil in a small saucepan (adding more stock or water if necessary) and stirring in ½ teaspoon cornflour mixed to a smooth paste with cold water. Pour over mushrooms on serving dish.

Steamed Stuffed Mushrooms

Cold Hors d'Oeuvres

0	I Crystal Cooked Chicken (page 97)
5	6 large Braised Mushrooms (page 140)
7	125 g (4 oz) Barbecued Pork Fillet (page 126)
2.3	I x 454 g (16 oz) can abalone
6	I cucumber
I	I large white radish or a few small red radishes
2	2 lap cheong (Chinese sausages)
	MARINADE
8	4 tablespoons light soy sauce
Tr	I tablespoon sherry
0	I tablespoon sesame oil
Tr	I teaspoon ginger juice
	spring onion (scallion) curls, radish fans or roses for garnish

32.3	**total grams carbohydrate**

There is very little carbohydrate per portion in this selection of hors d'oeuvres. The marinade has been adapted to the diet, leaving out the sugar it would normally contain, and in the recipe for braised mushrooms the amount of sugar has been substantially reduced.

Prepare the Crystal Cooked Chicken, Braised Mushrooms and Barbecued Pork Fillet a day in advance.

Drain abalone liquid and reserve for adding to a soup. Cut the abalone into paper thin slices and pour over them half the combined marinade ingredients.

Peel cucumber thinly, leaving a hint of green. Run a fork down the length of the cucumber to give a decorative edge, cut into very thin slices and spoon the rest of the marinade over the slices. Set aside.

Slice the radish thinly. The lap cheong is the only item that should not be cold, so steam it shortly before required, then cut into thin diagonal slices.

With a sharp knife cut chicken flesh from bone in two halves. Place on a board, skin side upwards, and slice thinly.

Cut the braised mushrooms in slices or quarters. Slice the pork fillet thinly.

Arrange the ingredients attractively on a serving platter, grouping them individually. Reserve marinade from the cucumber and abalone and serve as a dip, adding more soy sauce, sherry and sesame oil if necessary.

Barbecued Pork Fillet (see page 126)

Cold Hors d'Oeuvres

Cold Chicken in Oyster Sauce

0	1 whole chicken breast or half a roasting chicken
Tr	few celery leaves
6	1 small onion
0	1 teaspoon salt
6	1 teaspoon honey
2	1 tablespoon oyster sauce
2	1 tablespoon light soy sauce
0	⅛ teaspoon five spice powder
3	3 tablespoons finely chopped spring onion (scallion)
1	3 teaspoons finely grated fresh ginger
6	2 tablespoons toasted sesame seed
26.5	**total grams carbohydrate**

Put chicken breast or half chicken into a saucepan with just enough cold water to cover, add celery leaves, onion and salt for flavour, and bring slowly to the boil. Cover and simmer on very gentle heat for 10 minutes, turn off heat and allow chicken to cool in liquid. Cooling in the liquid ensures that chicken stays moist and flavoursome. Take chicken from liquid, remove all skin and bones and slice the meat thinly. Arrange on a plate.

In a bowl, mix together the honey, oyster sauce, soy sauce and spice powder, then spoon over the chicken. Cover and leave for 30 minutes. Before serving sprinkle all over with chopped spring onion and ginger mixed together, then with the sesame seed.

Note: To toast sesame seed put into a dry frying pan and shake or stir constantly over medium low heat for 5 minutes or until seeds are golden. Remove from pan immediately or they will darken and become bitter.

Cold Lemon Chicken with Fresh Coriander

Serves: *4 as a main dish,*
8-10 as part of an hors-d'oeuvres tray.

0	500 g (1 lb) chicken fillets or half a roasting chicken
Tr	few celery leaves
6	1 small onion
16	2 tablespoons Chinese lemon sauce
2	1 tablespoon dark soy sauce
1	3 tablespoons finely chopped fresh coriander leaves (cilantro) and stems
Tr	1 teaspoon finely grated fresh ginger
26	total grams carbohydrate

Cook chicken as per preceding recipe. Cool and slice as described.

Combine lemon sauce and soy sauce. Marinate chicken in this mixture at least 30 minutes, and arrange on serving dish. Sprinkle with finely chopped coriander and grated ginger mixed together.

Egg Foo Yong

2	4 eggs
0	½ teaspoon salt
6	1 cup fresh bean sprouts
6	3 spring onions (scallions), finely chopped, including green tops
0	peanut oil for frying
14	total grams carbohydrate

Usually served with sweet and sour sauce—but try these little omelettes with just a dash of soy sauce or vinegar for a new taste and no added carbohydrates.

Beat eggs with salt. Wash and drain sprouts well, removing any brown tails or loose skins. Add sprouts and spring onions to beaten egg. Lightly grease a heavy frying pan or wok with peanut oil. Pour in ¼ cup of the egg mixture. Cook until brown on underside, turn and cook other side. Repeat with remaining mixture. Stack 2 or 3 foo yong for each serving.

Egg Foo Yong

Egg Roll

Serves: 8 as part of a selection of hors d'oeuvres.

2.5	5 eggs
0	½ teaspoon salt
0	small pinch of pepper
0	1 tablespoon peanut oil
0	1 teaspoon sesame oil
	FILLING
0	185 g (6 oz) minced (ground) lean pork
0	½ teaspoon salt
0	pinch of pepper
2	1 tablespoon light soy sauce
0	½ teaspoon sesame oil
2.5	1 teaspoon cornflour (cornstarch)
Tr	3 teaspoons finely chopped fresh coriander (cilantro)
4	2 spring onions (scallions), finely chopped
11.5	total grams carbohydrate

Beat eggs well and add salt and pepper. Reserve a tablespoon of the beaten egg mixture for sealing the egg rolls. Heat a small omelette pan or wok and grease lightly with a little of the peanut oil and sesame oil mixed together. Pour about 2–3 tablespoons of the egg mixture into pan and swirl pan to make a thin omelette, cooking it on one side only. Turn onto a plate. Repeat with more oil and more of the egg mixture. There should be 4 or 5 omelettes, depending on the size of your pan. Divide filling into the same number of portions as there are omelettes.

Place each omelette on a board, cooked side up, and spread filling almost to the edge, using an oiled spatula or back of an oiled tablespoon. Roll up like a Swiss roll and seal edges of omelette with reserved beaten egg. Place on a plate lightly oiled with the same oil used for cooking the omelette.

Put plate in a steamer or on a rack in a saucepan of boiling water, cover and steam for 15 minutes. (The plate should be a little smaller than the steamer or pan to allow steam to circulate.) Remove from heat, cool slightly, then cut into diagonal slices and serve hot or cold as an hors d'oeuvre.

Filling: Put pork, salt, pepper and soy sauce in food processor or electric blender and blend until almost a paste. (If using a blender it will be necessary to switch motor on and off frequently, and move mixture onto the blades with a spatula.) Turn into a bowl, add other ingredients, combine well.

Egg Roll with Prawn Filling

Serves: *8 as part of a selection of hors d'oeuvres*

3	185 g (6 oz) raw prawns, shelled and de-veined
0	1 teaspoon salt
0	1 teaspoon sesame oil
2.5	1 teaspoon cornflour (cornstarch)
2	1 tablespoon finely chopped spring onions (scallions)
2.5	Omelettes as in previous recipe.
10	total grams carbohydrate

Chop prawns very finely and mix in other ingredients, proceed as in previous recipe for Egg Roll.

Marbled Tea Eggs

Serves: *12–18 as part of a selection of hors d'oeuvres*

3	6 eggs
0	4 cups water
0	3 tablespoons tea leaves
0	1 tablespoon salt
0	1 tablespoon five spice powder
3	total grams carbohydrate

Put eggs in a saucepan, cover with cold water and bring slowly to the boil, stirring gently to centre the yolks. Simmer for 7 minutes. Cool eggs thoroughly in cold water for 5 minutes. Lightly crack each eggshell by rolling on a hard surface until the shell is cracked all over. Do not remove the shell.

Bring 4 cups water to the boil, add tea leaves, salt and five spice powder. Add cracked eggs. Simmer, covered, for approximately 30 minutes or until shells turn brown. Let eggs stand in covered pan for at least 30 minutes, or overnight if possible. Drain, cool and shell. (The whites of eggs will have a marbled pattern on them.) Cut into quarters and serve with a dipping sauce.

Crab Omelette

Serves: 2

2	4 eggs
0	½ teaspoon salt
0	¼ teaspoon freshly ground black pepper
2	1 cup crab meat
0	extra salt and pepper for seasoning
1	squeeze of lemon juice
0	1 teaspoon peanut oil
0	1 teaspoon sesame oil
6	3 spring onions (scallions), finely chopped
0.8	1 green chilli, finely chopped
11.8	**total grams carbohydrate**

Beat eggs slightly, as for a French omelette. Season with salt and pepper. Season crab meat with salt and pepper to taste and add a squeeze of lemon juice. Grease a heavy omelette pan with oils and gently fry half the spring onions and chilli for a minute or two. Pour in half the beaten eggs and cook until set and golden on the bottom, creamy on top. Meanwhile heat crab meat in a separate pan. Spoon half the crab meat down the centre of the omelette and fold over once. Slide onto a plate and serve hot. Repeat with remaining mixtures to make a second omelette.

Seafood

This is the chapter I hope you will use most as you eat your way down to your ideal weight. Fish is healthy, high protein food that is good for you. It is also low in cholesterol. Shellfish is low in calories but high in cholesterol, so if you have a cholesterol problem use fish rather than shellfish.

As you leaf through you may look for restaurant favourites such as crumbed butterfly prawns, but you will not find them here. The reason is that the breadcrumb coating adds a hefty number of grams of carbohydrate per prawn, so it is obviously a recipe that has no place in this book. After all, why tempt you and turn your thoughts to this kind of food, then tell you that all you should have is half a prawn! If some recipes are conspicuously absent, there is a good reason.

Luxury ingredients such as abalone, lobster, scallops and crab are included. Not for everyday meals, but to give you the comfort of knowing that indulgence of the taste buds is allowed and will not stop you losing weight if the principles of the diet and the carefully calculated recipes are followed.

Steamed Fish, Sichuan-Style

Serves: 2–4

0	1 whole fish, about 750 g (1½ lb)
0	½ teaspoon salt
Tr	½ teaspoon finely grated fresh ginger
0	¼ cup liquid from fish
Tr	1 tablespoon sherry
1	1 teaspoon crushed garlic
1	1 teaspoon finely chopped fresh ginger
2	2 teaspoons chilli bean sauce
0	3 tablespoons peanut oil
0	1 teaspoon sesame oil
4	2 spring onions (scallions), finely sliced
1	2–3 tablespoons chopped fresh coriander (cilantro)
10	total grams carbohydrate

Wash, scale and clean fish. Rub over with salt and grated ginger, place in a lightly oiled heatproof dish and steam over boiling water for 8–10 minutes. Pour liquid that collects around fish into a measuring cup and add sherry. Mix garlic and chopped ginger into the chilli bean sauce. Heat peanut and sesame oils in wok and when very hot pour 2 tablespoons of it over the fish. Add bean sauce mixture to oil remaining in wok and stir-fry for 1 minute. Add mixed liquid and spring onions, bring to the boil and pour over the fish. Garnish with chopped coriander.

Steamed Fish with Mushroom Sauce

Serves: 2

2	4 dried Chinese mushrooms
0	1 tablespoon peanut oil
8	4 spring onions (scallions), chopped
Tr	½ teaspoon finely grated fresh ginger
2	1 tablespoon soy sauce
1	½ cup fish stock (see page 156)
2.5	1 teaspoon cornflour (cornstarch)
0	1 tablespoon cold water
0	500 g (1 lb) snapper or jewfish fillets
0	salt and pepper to taste
Tr	½ teaspoon finely grated fresh ginger
4	2 spring onions (scallions), sliced
20.5	total grams carbohydrate

Soak mushrooms in hot water for 30 minutes. Remove and discard stems, slice mushrooms finely. Heat oil and fry spring onions and ginger for a few seconds, then add soy sauce and fish stock mixed together. Bring to the boil, stir in cornflour mixed with cold water and stir until clear and thickened. Keep sauce warm while preparing fish.

Wash and dry fish fillets. Remove skin. Season with salt and pepper and rub all over with the ginger. Put fillets on a plate rubbed with a little sesame oil, top with sliced mushrooms and spring onions and steam over boiling water for 8–10 minutes. Pour sauce over fish and serve.

Steamed Fish Fillets with Crab Sauce

Serves: 2

0	500 g (1 lb) fillets of bream or other white fish
Tr	½ teaspoon finely grated fresh ginger
0	1 teaspoon salt
Tr	1 teaspoon light soy sauce

SAUCE

0	1 tablespoon peanut oil
6	3 spring onions (scallions), chopped
Tr	½ teaspoon finely grated fresh ginger
0	liquid from steamed fish
1	125 g (4 oz) crab meat
0	pinch of pepper
2.5	1 teaspoon cornflour (cornstarch)
0	1 tablespoon cold water
11	**total grams carbohydrate**

With a sharp knife, remove skin from fish. To do this sprinkle a little salt on the end of the fillet near the tail to enable it to be grasped without slipping. Then slide a knife between the skin and flesh, working towards the head of the fish. Wash fish and pat dry. Lay the fillets on a chopping board and rub with the grated ginger, salt and soy sauce. Place in a heatproof dish and steam for 8 minutes over simmering water. Remove from heat and pour liquid from dish into a measuring cup. Make up to ½ cup with added water.

Sauce: Heat oil and gently fry spring onions and ginger for a few seconds, stirring, then add fish liquid, cover and simmer for 3–4 minutes. Add crab meat, heat through for not longer than a minute. Season with pepper. Mix cornflour smoothly with the cold water and stir into sauce. Continue stirring over medium heat until sauce boils and thickens. Taste, and add salt if necessary. Arrange fish fillets on a dish, spoon sauce over and serve at once.

Steamed Fish with Chilli Oil

Serves: 2–4

0	I whole fish, about I kg (2 lb)
0	½ teaspoon salt
Tr	½ teaspoon finely grated fresh ginger
Tr	I tablespoon sherry
0	sesame oil
4	2 tablespoons light soy sauce
0	I teaspoon chilli oil
Tr	I teaspoon ginger juice
0	I teaspoon sesame oil
0	2 tablespoons peanut oil
Tr	sprigs of fresh coriander (cilantro) for garnish
6	**total grams carbohydrate**

Wash and clean fish and rub inside and out with salt, grated ginger and sherry. Oil a heatproof dish with sesame oil and place the fish on it. Steam over gently boiling water for 8–10 minutes or until fish is cooked. In a small bowl combine the soy sauce, chilli oil, ginger juice and sesame oil. While fish is cooking, heat the peanut oil. Pour sizzling hot oil over the fish, add the combined seasonings and serve, garnished with sprigs of fresh coriander. Serve extra chilli oil or soy chilli sauce dip for those who like very hot flavours.

Note: For ginger juice, grate fresh ginger finely, then press out juice through a fine nylon sieve.

Steamed Snapper Fillets with Black Beans

Serves: 2–4

0	2 large or 4 medium snapper fillets
0	½ teaspoon salt
Tr	½ teaspoon grated fresh ginger
Tr	½ teaspoon crushed garlic
2	1 spring onion (scallion), cut in thin diagonal slices
2	2 teaspoons canned salted black beans, rinsed
Tr	2 teaspoons light soy sauce
Tr	1 tablespoon dry sherry
Tr	chilli or spring onion flowers for garnish
6.5	**total grams carbohydrate**

Wash and dry fish fillets, then rub over with salt, grated ginger and crushed garlic. Place on an oiled heatproof plate. Place spring onion slices and rinsed black beans over the fillets, then mix the soy sauce and sherry together and spoon over the fish. Steam over gently boiling water for 8–10 minutes, depending on the size of the fillets. Serve at once, garnished with chilli or spring onion flowers.

Steamed Ocean Perch with Brown Bean Sauce

Serves: 2

0	500 g (1 lb) fillets of ocean perch or 1 whole perch, about 1 kg (2 lb)
Tr	½ teaspoon finely grated fresh ginger
0	½ teaspoon salt
3	1 tablespoon brown bean sauce (min sze jeung)
Tr	1 tablespoon sherry
1	2 thin slices ginger
Tr	1 clove garlic
6	3 spring onions (scallions)
0	2 tablespoons peanut oil

11.5	total grams carbohydrate

Wash and dry the fish fillets. If using whole fish make sure all scales are removed, trim the fins and spines but leave the head on. Wipe out cavity with a damp paper towel dipped in coarse salt and rinse. Dry fish with a paper towel. Rub fish with grated ginger and salt. Combine the bean sauce and sherry. Cut the slices of ginger into thread-like strips and finely chop the garlic. Slice spring onions finely.

Put the fish in a heatproof dish and place over boiling water, cover and steam for 5 minutes if using fillets, 8–10 minutes if using a whole fish. Liquid that collects in the dish should be added to the bean sauce and sherry mixture.

Heat the oil in a wok and fry the ginger, garlic and spring onions, stirring constantly, for 1 minute. Add the sauce mixture and bring to the boil, simmer on low heat for a further minute and spoon over the fish. Serve at once.

Steamed Fish Balls with Snow Peas

Steamed Fish Balls with Snow Peas

Serves: 2

0	375 g (12 oz) fillets of fish
Tr	¼ teaspoon finely grated fresh ginger
Tr	1 clove garlic, crushed
Tr	½ teaspoon salt
Tr	1 egg yolk
2.5	1 teaspoon cornflour (cornstarch)
0	1 tablespoon peanut oil
12	125 g (4 oz) snow peas, strings removed
1	½ cup fish or chicken stock (see page 156)
2.5	1 teaspoon cornflour (cornstarch)
0	1 tablespoon cold water
2	1 tablespoon oyster sauce
2	½ teaspoon sugar
24	**total grams carbohydrate**

This dish cannot be made with cooked fish. If snow peas are not available, substitute broccoli, sliced celery, or sliced Chinese mustard cabbage.

Remove skin and bones from fish and chop very finely. Combine with ginger, garlic, salt, egg yolk and 1 teaspoon cornflour. Lightly grease hands with sesame oil and form the fish into small balls about 2.5 cm (1 in) across. Place the balls on a plate, put plate on a rack and steam over gently boiling water in a covered pan for 10 minutes.

When fish balls are cooked, heat peanut oil in the wok, and on high heat, toss the snow peas in the oil until they turn bright green. This takes about 2 minutes. Push peas to side of wok, pour in stock, add remaining teaspoon cornflour mixed with water and cook, stirring, until clear and thickened, about 1 minute. Stir in oyster sauce and sugar. Stir snow peas into the sauce.

Arrange fish balls on a dish, spoon snow peas and sauce over and serve immediately.

Steamed Fish with Ham and Bamboo Shoots

Serves: 2–4

0	750 g (1½ lb) fillets of blue eye cod, snapper, pearl perch or other white fish
0	½ teaspoon salt
Tr	1 teaspoon ginger juice
2	6 dried Chinese mushrooms
2	1 tablespoon light soy sauce
0	2 teaspoons sesame oil
8	2 teaspoons sugar
1	2 tablespoons dry sherry
1	1 tablespoon finely shredded fresh ginger
4	3 tablespoons each bamboo shoot and cooked ham cut into matchstick strips
3	2 spring onions (scallions), cut into matchstick strips
Tr	sprigs of fresh coriander or spring onion flowers for garnish
22	**total grams carbohydrate**

Make this elegant dish with a larger fish for a party, allowing more time for the fish to cook and increasing the other ingredients accordingly.

Wash and clean the fish, wipe with paper, rub inside and out with salt and ginger juice. Set aside while preparing mushrooms. Wash and soak mushrooms in hot water for 20 minutes, discard stems and cut caps into thin strips. Put the mushroom strips in a small pan with the soy sauce, sesame oil, sugar and ½ cup of the mushroom soaking water. Bring to the boil, then cover and simmer for 10 minutes. Drain the mushroom strips and add the sherry to the liquid left in the pan.

Lightly oil a heatproof dish and put half the strips of ginger, bamboo, ham, mushrooms and spring onions (scallions) on the dish. Place the fish on them and spread the remaining ingredients over the fish. Place the dish over gently boiling water, cover and steam for 12–15 minutes or until the fish is cooked. Pour the sherry mixture over the fish, garnish with sprigs of fresh coriander or spring onion flowers and serve at once. After the top half of the fish has been served, lift the backbone and snap it off near the head, then serve the bottom half of the fish together with the ingredients underneath it and the juices in the dish.

Note: To make ginger juice, grate fresh ginger finely then press out juice through a fine nylon sieve.

Steamed Fish with Ham and Bamboo Shoots

Steamed Pearl Perch with Walnuts

Serves: 4

0	1 whole pearl perch or other white fish about 1 kg (2 lb)
0	salt
1	1 teaspoon finely grated fresh ginger
4	2 tablespoons light soy sauce
0	¼ cup peanut oil
4	¼ cup peeled walnuts
0	1 teaspoon sesame oil
6	3 spring onions (scallions), thinly sliced
15	**total grams carbohydrate**

Clean and scale fish, but leave head and tail on. Dip a piece of dampened paper towel in salt and clean out the cavity of the fish carefully. Rinse well. Trim fins and sharp spines with kitchen scissors. Rub fish all over, inside and out, with the ginger and 1 tablespoon soy sauce. Place on a heatproof dish, put dish on steaming rack in wok, add 3 cups boiling water, cover the wok and steam the fish for 10–12 minutes, or until fish is cooked. Test at the thickest part and if flesh is opaque the fish is done.

Lift dish from steamer, cover with foil and keep warm. Dry the wok well, heat oil and fry the walnuts over medium heat just until pale golden. (Peeled walnuts are sometimes available at Chinese stores and are preferable to ordinary walnuts because there is no thin skin to give a bitter taste.)

Lift out walnuts on slotted spoon and drain on absorbent paper. Take 3 tablespoons of the hot oil and pour over the fish. Combine remaining tablespoon soy sauce and sesame oil and pour over the fish also. Garnish with the walnuts and sliced spring onions and serve, accompanied by rice.

Boiled Whole Fish, Honan-Style

Serves: 2

0	1 x 500 g (1 lb) fresh snapper, ocean perch or other whole white fish
0	1 teaspoon salt
0	1 tablespoon peanut oil
1	1 teaspoon finely grated fresh ginger
16	8 spring onions (scallions), finely chopped
0	1 teaspoon sesame oil
4	2 tablespoons light soy sauce
21	total grams carbohydrate

To serve 4, use a larger fish. Increase seasonings and cooking time accordingly.

Scale, clean and wash fish and trim spines and fins but leave head and tail on. Put enough water into a wok or frying pan to cover the fish (but do not add fish yet), add salt, bring to the boil and lower the fish into it, cover and return to the boil. Reduce heat and cook 5–7 minutes. Remove from liquid and drain well.

Heat peanut oil in a small saucepan and fry ginger and spring onions very gently until soft but not brown. Remove from heat. Add sesame oil and soy sauce. Put fish on a serving dish (on a bed of stir-fried lettuce if liked—see page 150). Spoon the sauce over and serve at once.

Boiled Fish, Sichuan-Style

0	I whole fish, about I kg (2 lb)
2	4 dried Chinese mushrooms
4	2 spring onions (scallions)
Tr	I tablespoon sherry
2	2 teaspoons bean sauce (min sze jeung)
Tr	2 teaspoons vinegar
0	I tablespoon peanut oil
I	I teaspoon finely grated fresh ginger
Tr	½ teaspoon crushed garlic
10.5	**total grams carbohydrate**

Choose a firm, white-fleshed fish for this dish—snapper, pearl perch, ocean perch or similar fish are suitable.

Clean and scale fish, but leave head on. Trim fins and tail with kitchen scissors, make 3 or 4 diagonal slashes on each side of fish half-way to the bone. Soak the dried mushrooms in hot water for 20 minutes, discard stems and cut caps into fine slices. Cut spring onions into thin diagonal slices. Combine the sherry, bean sauce and vinegar in a small bowl with 2 tablespoons of the mushroom water and set aside.

Heat enough water in a wok to cover the fish and when it is boiling lower the fish in, cover with lid and allow to just simmer for 4 –5 minutes. Turn off heat and leave covered in the water for 15 minutes. Drain fish and remove to a serving dish.

While fish is cooking in the stored heat, prepare the sauce. Heat peanut oil and on fairly low heat fry the ginger and garlic until just turning golden. Add the mushrooms and spring onions and fry for another minute, stirring. Add all the mixed seasonings, bring to the boil and pour over the fish. Garnish with spring onion curls and serve at once.

Grilled Fish with Chilli Bean Sauce

Serves: 2-4

0	1 whole perch, snapper or bream about 1 kg (2 lb)
0	½ teaspoon salt
Tr	½ teaspoon finely grated fresh ginger
0	1 teaspoon sesame oil
0	1 tablespoon peanut oil
1	1 tablespoon finely shredded fresh ginger
Tr	1 clove garlic, crushed
2	1 tablespoon light soy sauce
2	2 teaspoons chilli bean sauce
6	3 spring onions (scallions), cut into bite-sized lengths
0	3 tablespoons water
12	**total grams carbohydrate**

For those who like hot flavours, this recipe will become a favourite.

Clean and wash fish, dry with paper towels and cut two or three diagonal slashes on each side. Rub over with salt and ginger, brush with sesame oil, making sure it goes into the slashes. Place fish on foil-lined griller pan.

Grill fish on both sides under pre-heated griller until cooked, testing with tip of knife at thickest part. When flesh is white and opaque, it is done. Do not cook for too long or it will be dry.

While fish is cooking, heat the peanut oil in a small pan and fry the ginger and garlic on low heat until just starting to colour. Add the remaining ingredients, bring to the boil and pour over the fish before serving.

Deep-Fried Fish, Sichuan Style

Serves: 2 as a main dish

0	1 whole firm white-fleshed fish about 750 g (1½ lb)
1	2 tablespoons Chinese wine or dry sherry
2	1 tablespoon light soy sauce
2.5	1 teaspoon cornflour (cornstarch)
0	1 tablespoon cold water
2	1 tablespoon dark soy sauce
2	½ teaspoon sugar
0	¼ cup peanut oil for frying
1	2 teaspoons finely grated fresh ginger
1	3 cloves garlic, finely chopped or grated
4	1 tablespoon hot bean sauce (see Glossary, page 179)
0	½ cup water
4	2 spring onions (scallions), finely chopped
18.5	**total grams carbohydrate**

Clean the fish thoroughly, leaving head and tail on. Trim spines with kitchen scissors. Wash well and dry on paper towels. With a sharp knife or chopper score the fish length-ways, making parallel cuts about a finger's width apart and almost through to the bone to allow seasonings to penetrate. Combine 2 tablespoons wine and light soy sauce and marinate the fish in the mixture, making sure it goes in all the cuts.

Mix cornflour with cold water, then stir in dark soy sauce, remaining wine and the sugar. Set aside.

Heat peanut oil in a wok or large frying pan until very hot. Drain away marinade, add fish, and deep fry about 3–4 minutes on each side or until the fish is golden brown. Turn fish once only when cooking. Drain on slotted spoon and put fish on a heated serving platter. Pour off oil in wok, leaving about 2 tablespoons, and fry the ginger and garlic over medium heat, stirring constantly, until garlic starts to turn golden. Add the bean sauce and stir, then add water. Stir the sauce ingredients once more to distribute the cornflour evenly, add to wok and stir constantly until mixture comes to the boil, becomes clear and thickens slightly. Add spring onions and stir well. Pour sauce over fish and serve immediately with rice.

Fillets of Fish in Black Bean Sauce

Serves: 2

0	500 g (1 lb) fillets of firm white fish
10	1 tablespoon cornflour
2	2 tablespoons canned salted black beans
1	2 cloves garlic
4	1 teaspoon sugar
1	1 teaspoon finely grated fresh ginger
0	½ cup water
Tr	2 tablespoons dry sherry
2.5	1 teaspoon cornflour (cornstarch)
0	3 tablespoons peanut oil
4	2 spring onions (scallions), cut in thin diagonal slices
25	**total grams carbohydrate**

Served with a vegetable dish, there is no need for rice or other starch fillers.

Wash and dry fish. Cut in two lengthways, then cut each piece across into finger-size strips. Leave the narrow tail end of the fillets in bite-sized pieces. Dust the pieces with the cornflour. Rinse the black beans in a strainer under the cold tap, put on a wooden board and chop or mash with a fork. Crush garlic with the sugar and mix with the ginger and the beans. Combine water, sherry and cornflour in a cup.

Heat wok, add peanut oil and when hot put in the pieces of fish, a few at a time, and fry for 1 minute or until colour changes. Drain on slotted spoon. Cook rest of fish, adding more oil if necessary. In 1 tablespoon oil, fry the black bean mixture for 1 minute. Stir the water, sherry and cornflour until smooth and add to pan. Stir constantly until it boils and thickens slightly. Add fish pieces and spring onions, heat through and serve.

Fish Fillets with Hoi Sin Sauce

0	375 g (12 oz) white fish fillets
0	2 tablespoons peanut oil
Tr	1 clove garlic, bruised
2	1 tablespoon light soy sauce
Tr	½ teaspoon finely grated fresh ginger
2	1 teaspoon hoi sin sauce
2	spring onion (scallion) strips for garnish
7	total grams carbohydrate

Remove skins from fish fillets, wash and dry well on paper towels. Heat oil in wok, fry garlic until golden, remove and discard. Add the fillets, one at a time, turning after a few seconds and moving to side of wok to make room for the next. When all the fish has been added to the wok sprinkle with soy sauce, cover with lid and simmer for 1 minute. Add ginger to liquid in pan, cover and simmer 1 minute more. Remove from heat, stir in hoi sin sauce. Arrange fish on serving platter, spoon sauce over, garnish with spring onion strips and serve hot.

Red Cooked Fish

0	1 whole fish, about 1.5 kg (3 lb)
0	1 teaspoon salt
20	2 tablespoons cornflour (cornstarch)
0	1 teaspoon five spice powder
0	⅛ teaspoon pepper
6	¼ cup dark soy sauce
Tr	2 tablespoons dry sherry
0	1 cup water
0	2 teaspoons sesame oil
8	2 teaspoons sugar
0	6 tablespoons peanut oil for frying
1	6 thin slices fresh ginger
1	2 cloves garlic, bruised
0	1 whole star anise
4	2 spring onions (scallions), cut into short lengths
1.25	½ teaspoon cornflour (cornstarch)
0	2 teaspoons cold water
Tr	spring onion flowers or sprigs of fresh coriander (cilantro) for garnish

42.25   total grams carbohydrate

Red cooked dishes must have a little sugar to impart the right flavour. The carbohydrates for each serving won't amount to very much, because the entire quantity of sauce is not served.

Wash and clean fish, leaving head on. Wipe dry with paper towels. Score the fish lightly, no more than half-way to the bone, making three or four diagonal slashes on each side. Combine the salt, cornflour, five spice powder and pepper by sifting together. Rub the mixture over the fish to coat lightly and dust off excess. Combine liquid ingredients and stir in sugar until dissolved.

Heat a wok, pour in the peanut oil and allow the oil time to heat. Lower the fish carefully into the oil and fry over high heat for 2 minutes or until underside of fish is golden brown. Turn the fish, using a large spatula under the thickest part of the fish and helping it with a second spatula. Cook on the second side for a further 2 minutes or until golden. Pour off the oil. Add the soy sauce mixture, pouring it over the fish. Add ginger, garlic, star anise, spring onions. Lower heat to let the liquid merely simmer gently. Cover and cook for 10–12 minutes, basting two or three times with the sauce. Test at thickest part of fish with point of a knife. If flesh is milky white and flakes easily, the fish is cooked.

Carefully lift fish onto a serving plate. Strain sauce left in pan. (This 'master sauce' can be used for cooking other seafoods and keeps for months in the freezer.) Heat ½ cup of the sauce, stir in ½ teaspoon cornflour mixed with 2 teaspoons cold water. When sauce boils and thickens slightly, pour over the fish and serve, garnished with spring onion flowers or sprigs of fresh coriander.

Velvet Fish with Oyster Sauce

0	375 g (12 oz) fillet of snapper or gemfish
0	½ teaspoon salt
0	pinch pepper
2.5	1 teaspoon cornflour (cornstarch)
0	3 tablespoons peanut oil
0	1 tablespoon egg white
Tr	½ teaspoon finely grated fresh ginger
8	4 spring onions (scallions), cut into bite-sized pieces
4	2 tablespoons oyster sauce
15	**total grams carbohydrate**

Skin fillet and cut into bite-sized pieces. Season with salt and pepper, set aside for 10 minutes. Sprinkle with cornflour and 1 tablespoon of the peanut oil, mix well to coat fish pieces and leave for 15 minutes. Add egg white, mix again and chill for 30 minutes.

Bring about 5 cups water to the boil, add a tablespoon of peanut oil to the water and drop in the fish pieces. Return to the boil and cook for 1 minute, then drain.

Heat a wok, add remaining tablespoon oil and swirl to coat inside of wok. Add ginger and spring onions and stir-fry on high heat for 1 minute. Add oyster sauce and stir, add the fish pieces and heat through. Serve at once.

Note: The fish may be prepared hours beforehand, or even a day ahead, up to the point where it is drained. It is then only a few minutes work to heat and assemble the dish.

Stir-Fried Fish Cake and Cabbage

Serves: 2

5	1 prepared fish cake or 250 g (8 oz) white fish fillet
4	2 cups sliced mustard cabbage
0	1 tablespoon peanut oil
2	1 finely chopped spring onion
Tr	½ teaspoon crushed garlic
Tr	½ teaspoon finely grated fresh ginger
2	1 tablespoon oyster sauce
2	1 tablespoon light soy sauce
0	¼ cup hot water
2.5	1 teaspoon cornflour (cornstarch)
0	1 tablespoon cold water
18.5	**total grams carbohydrate**

Mustard cabbage or gai choy gives this dish a distinctive tang, but if not available use one of the other types of Chinese cabbage. Fish cakes sold at Chinese stores are convenient to use but contain a proportion of cornflour, so you can substitute fish fillets and cut the carbohydrate content of the recipe by 5 grams.

Slice the fish cake or fillet very thinly and cut the slices in halves so they are bite-sized. Slice the mustard cabbage in thick slices, keeping the leafy portion separate from the stems. Heat peanut oil and fry the finely chopped spring onion over medium low heat until soft. Add garlic and ginger and stir for a few seconds, then add the stems of the mustard cabbage and stir-fry for 1 minute. Add oyster sauce, soy sauce and water, cover and simmer for 1 minute. Add fish slices and leafy portion of mustard cabbage and heat through. Mix cornflour to a smooth paste with a tablespoon of cold water, stir into liquid and bring to the boil, stirring until it thickens slightly. Serve immediately.

Baked Snapper Stuffed with Pork

*Serves: 2 as a main dish,
4 with other courses*

0	1 medium-sized snapper (about 1.5 kg (3 lb)
0	1 teaspoon salt
1	1 teaspoon finely grated fresh ginger
0	125 g (4 oz) pork mince (ground pork)
Tr	1 clove garlic, crushed
1.5	1 tablespoon finely chopped spring onion (scallion)
0	¼ teaspoon salt
0	⅛ teaspoon pepper
6	¼ cup dark soy sauce
Tr	2 tablespoons dry sherry
0	1 cup water
0	2 teaspoons sesame oil
8	2 teaspoons sugar
1	6 thin slices fresh ginger
1	2 cloves garlic, bruised
0	1 whole star anise
2	1 spring onion (scallion), cut into pieces
22	**total grams carbohydrate**

If you have Master Sauce left from Red Cooked Chicken (page 95) or Red Cooked Fish (page 51), use 1 cup instead of the soy sauce, sherry and flavourings.

Wash and clean fish thoroughly, leaving head on. Cut slashes on either side of fish and rub over with 1 teaspoon salt and half the grated ginger.

Combine pork with remaining ginger, the crushed garlic, chopped spring onion, salt and pepper. Fill the cavity of the fish with the pork mixture and place it in an oiled baking dish. Combine all the other ingredients and pour over the fish. Bake in a moderate oven 30–35 minutes or until fish is cooked, basting frequently with the sauce.

Lift fish onto serving platter and spoon some of the sauce over. Garnish with sprigs of fresh coriander or spring onion flowers and serve hot.

Note: If preferred the fish may be braised instead of baked. First fry for 2 minutes on each side in 6 tablespoons of peanut oil. Pour off oil and add sauce. Cover and simmer for 7 minutes on one side, then turn fish carefully and simmer for 15 minutes on the other side. Make sure liquid is sufficient to half cover the fish so that pork filling in cavity is submerged. If necessary add more water.

Braised Fish and Prawn Rolls

Serves: 2–4

4	12 raw prawns (shrimp)
0	500 g (1 lb) firm white fish fillets
0	2 tablespoons peanut oil
1	3 thin slices fresh ginger
0	¼ cup hot water
2	1 tablespoon light soy sauce
Tr	1 tablespoon dry sherry
6	3 spring onions (scallions), sliced finely

13.5	total grams carbohydrate

Shell, de-vein and chop prawns with 1 slice ginger and ½ teaspoon salt. Form 12 portions. Remove skin and any bones from fish fillets and cut into 12 strips, each large enough to roll round a portion of prawn. Fasten with wooden toothpicks.

Heat peanut oil in wok, add slices of ginger and fry until they turn golden. Add fish rolls and fry for 2 minutes, turning them carefully with chopsticks or tongs. Add hot water, soy sauce and sherry. Cover and simmer for 5 minutes. Remove fish rolls to serving dish, add spring onions and stir. Remove and discard slices of ginger and pour sauce over fish. Garnish as desired and serve at once.

Fried Prawn Balls with Celery

Serves: 4

8	500 g (1 lb) raw prawns (shrimp)
Tr	½ teaspoon crushed garlic
Tr	½ teaspoon finely grated fresh ginger
0	¾ teaspoon salt
7.5	3 teaspoons cornflour (cornstarch)
2	1 stalk celery
2	1 tablespoon oyster sauce
1	2 teaspoons light soy sauce
0	3 tablespoons water
0	peanut oil for deep frying
Tr	3 thin slices fresh ginger
22	**total grams carbohydrate**

De-vein and chop prawns finely. Combine chopped prawns with the garlic, ginger, salt and two teaspoons cornflour. With oiled hands, form into small balls. Slice the celery fairly thinly, holding the knife at a 45 degree angle to give crescent shapes. Blanch the celery for 30–40 seconds in lightly salted boiling water until colour intensifies. Drain at once and refresh in iced water to set the colour. Drain once more and set aside. Measure out sauces, combining them in a small bowl with the 3 tablespoons of water and remaining teaspoon cornflour.

Heat peanut oil in a wok and fry the prawn balls, a few at a time, until pale golden. Drain on paper towels.

Pour oil from wok, leaving about a tablespoonful. On high heat fry the slices of ginger until golden, then add the celery crescents and stir-fry for 1 minute. Add the sauce and cornflour mixture and stir until liquid boils and thickens slightly, add prawn balls and toss together. Serve at once.

Prawn Balls with Bamboo Shoots

Serves: 2

4	250 g (8 oz) raw prawns
Tr	½ teaspoon finely grated fresh ginger
0	½ teaspoon salt
Tr	1 egg yolk
2.5	1 teaspoon cornflour (cornstarch)
7.5	1 x 400 g (14 oz) can braised bamboo shoots
1	½ cup stock from prawns (shrimp)
2	1 tablespoon soy sauce
2	1 tablespoon oyster sauce
2.5	1 teaspoon extra cornflour (cornstarch), optional
22.5	**total grams carbohydrate**

Shell and de-vein prawns and chop finely. Combine in a bowl with ginger, salt, egg yolk and half the cornflour. With oiled hands form into small balls. Bring about 1½ cups water to the boil in a medium saucepan, put in prawn balls and simmer gently for 10 minutes. Drain prawn balls, reserving the liquid for stock, and keep the prawn balls warm.

In another pan heat bamboo shoots with ½ cup of the prawn stock mixed with the soy and oyster sauce. If a thicker sauce is desired, stir in remaining 1 teaspoon cornflour mixed with a little cold water and allow to boil. Combine with the prawn balls, serve with ½ cup portions of rice or noodles.

Fried Prawns with Ginger

Serves: 2

4	250 g (8 oz) large raw prawns (jumbo shrimp)
Tr	½ teaspoon finely grated fresh ginger
2.5	1 teaspoon cornflour (cornstarch)
0	½ teaspoon salt
0	peanut oil for deep frying
1	lemon wedges for serving
8	total grams carbohydrate

Shell and de-vein prawns, wash and drain well or blot water with paper towels. Rub ginger well into prawns. Sprinkle cornflour and salt over prawns and mix well.

Heat oil in a wok or frying pan and when very hot, drop in a few prawns at a time. Fry quickly until they change colour, then lift out with a slotted spoon or Chinese wire strainer, drain on absorbent paper and serve hot with wedges of lemon. Each batch of prawns will need to be fried only 2 to 3 minutes. Do not over-cook or they will be tough and dry.

Prawns with Oyster Sauce

Serves: 2

4	250 g (8 oz) raw shelled prawns (shrimp)
4	2 stalks white celery
0	1 tablespoon peanut oil
Tr	½ teaspoon finely grated fresh ginger
2	½ cup sliced red capsicum (sweet pepper)
6	½ cup short lengths of spring onion (scallion) leaves
4	2 tablespoons oyster sauce
20.5	total grams carbohydrate

De-vein prawns, rinse and dry thoroughly on paper towels. Cut the celery into thin diagonal slices.

Heat the peanut oil in a wok and stir-fry the prawns and ginger for 2 minutes. Add celery, capsicum and spring onion leaves and fry for 1 minute longer on high heat. Add oyster sauce, turn heat low, cover and cook for 1 minute or until prawns are cooked through. Serve hot.

Prawns and Mushrooms in Black Bean Sauce

Serves: 2

6	12 raw prawns (shrimp)
2	4 dried Chinese mushrooms
1	1 tablespoon canned salted black beans
1	2 tablespoons Chinese wine or dry sherry
Tr	1 clove garlic, crushed
Tr	½ teaspoon finely grated fresh ginger
4	1 teaspoon sugar
0	1 teaspoon peanut oil
0	2 teaspoons sesame oil
2.5	1 teaspoon cornflour (cornstarch)
0	2 tablespoons water
17.5	**total grams carbohydrate**

Shell and de-vein prawns. Soak mushrooms in hot water for 30 minutes, cut off and discard stems, slice mushrooms finely. Put black beans into a small sieve and rinse under running cold water for a few seconds, drain and mash with a fork. It is easiest to do this on a wooden board. Put mashed beans into a bowl and mix with wine, garlic, ginger and sugar.

Heat peanut and sesame oils in a wok, add prawns and mushroom slices and stir-fry for 1 minute. Add bean mixture, lower heat, cover and simmer for 5 minutes. Add cornflour mixed smoothly with cold water, return to boil and stir until slightly thickened.

Serve immediately with ½ cup portions of rice or noodles, if preferred.

Prawns in Chilli Bean Sauce

Serves: 2–3

6	12 large raw prawns (jumbo shrimp)
Tr	1 clove garlic, crushed
0	½ teaspoon salt
Tr	½ teaspoon finely grated fresh ginger
Tr	2 teaspoons Chinese wine or dry sherry
3	1 red capsicum (sweet pepper)
3	1 green capsicum (sweet pepper)
4	1 tablespoon canned salted black beans
Tr	1–2 teaspoons Chinese chilli sauce
4	2 teaspoons hoi sin sauce
0	2 tablespoons peanut oil
Tr	spring onion (scallion) and chilli flowers to garnish
20	**total grams carbohydrate**

Shell and de-vein prawns, then put in a bowl and mix in garlic crushed with the salt. Add ginger and wine and leave to marinate while preparing other ingredients.

Cut capsicums in small squares. Rinse black beans and drain, then crush or chop finely and mix with chilli sauce and hoi sin sauce. Pour oil into a heated wok, stir-fry capsicums for 2 minutes, then push them to the side of the wok and add prawns to the oil. Fry over high heat until they turn pink, about 2 minutes. Move prawns to one side and add about half a tablespoon of oil. Add black bean and sauce mixture to oil and stir over heat for 30 seconds, then mix the prawns and capsicum into the sauce and fry for a few seconds until coated with the black bean mixture. Garnish and serve at once with ½ cup portions of rice.

Stir-Fried Prawns and Chinese Cabbage

Serves: 2

6	12 large raw prawns (jumbo shrimp)
4	1 Chinese cabbage (choy sum or gai choy)
0	¼ cup water or stock
2	1 tablespoon light soy sauce
0	¼ teaspoon five spice powder
Tr	1 tablespoon sherry or Chinese wine
0	½ teaspoon salt
2.5	1 teaspoon cornflour (cornstarch)
0	1 tablespoon cold water
0	2 tablespoons peanut oil
Tr	1 clove garlic, crushed
Tr	½ teaspoon finely grated fresh ginger

16.5	total grams carbohydrate

Shell and de-vein prawns. Cut cabbage into bite-sizedd pieces, using the thick stems and only the tender part of the leaves. In a small bowl combine the water or stock, soy sauce, five spice, sherry and salt. In a separate bowl mix cornflour with cold water.

Heat oil in a wok. Add garlic, ginger and cabbage and fry for 2 minutes over high heat, stirring constantly. Add prawns and fry for another minute. Lower heat to medium, add mixed seasonings, cover and simmer for 5 minutes. Add cornflour mixture and stir until sauce boils and thickens, about 1 minute. Serve at once with ½ cup portions of rice or noodles.

Note: If prawns are small, simmer for only 2 minutes.

Sichuan-Style Prawns with Dried Chillies

Serves: 6

8	500 g (1 lb) raw prawns (shrimp)
0	1 cup cold water
0	½ teaspoon salt
5	2 teaspoons cornflour (cornstarch)
0	1 tablespoon water
Tr	½ egg white, beaten slightly
0	½ teaspoon salt

SEASONINGS AND SAUCE

0	3 tablespoons peanut oil
Tr	8–10 large dried chillies
2.5	1 teaspoon cornflour (cornstarch)
0	2 teaspoons cold water
2	1 tablespoon light soy sauce
Tr	2 teaspoons Chinese wine or dry sherry
6	1½ teaspoons honey or sugar
Tr	1 teaspoon white vinegar
0	½ teaspoon salt
0	¼ teaspoon black pepper
4	2 spring onions (scallions), finely chopped
Tr	1 teaspoon grated or chopped fresh ginger
1	2 cloves garlic, crushed
31	**total grams carbohydrate**

Shell and de-vein prawns, put into a bowl and add cold water and salt. Stir and leave for 2 minutes, then rinse under cold tap for 1 minute. Drain well.

Make the marinade by mixing cornflour with cold water then adding egg white and salt. Add prawns, mix well, chill for 30 minutes.

Prepare seasonings and sauce. Break or cut tops off chillies, shake out and discard seeds.

Start cooking about 5 minutes before serving, for this is one dish that must be served immediately it is cooked. Heat a wok over medium heat, add the oil and heat again, swirling wok to coat inside with oil. Fry the chillies over medium heat until they are almost black. This takes only a few seconds, and they should be stirred and turned constantly. Remove chillies from wok and drain on absorbent paper. Mix cornflour and water in small bowl, then stir in light soy sauce, wine, honey, vinegar, salt and pepper. Set aside.

Drain any excess marinade from prawns, add prawns to wok and stir-fry over high heat. The prawns must not be over-cooked. Ten to 20 seconds is enough for very small prawns, 35 to 40 seconds for large prawns. Add spring onions, ginger and garlic and stir-fry briefly. Stir seasoning mixture again to blend the cornflour smoothly, add to the wok, stirring constantly until sauce boils and thickens. Turn off heat. Return chillies to the wok, stir to mix and serve immediately with ½ cup portions of rice.

Note: For a less hot result, discard oil in which the chillies are fried and heat fresh oil for frying the rest of the ingredients.

Prawns with Broccoli

Serves: 4

8	12–16 large raw prawns (jumbo shrimp)
10	1 head firm, fresh broccoli
0	1 tablespoon peanut oil
Tr	½ teaspoon finely grated fresh ginger
0	¼ teaspoon salt
0	4 tablespoons water
Tr	1 tablespoon Chinese wine or dry sherry
2.5	1 teaspoon cornflour (cornstarch)
0	1 tablespoon cold water
Tr	1 tablespoon shredded red chilli
	for garnish, optional
22	total grams carbohydrate

Shell and de-vein prawns, leaving tails on. With point of a sharp knife make a small slit through each prawn from the underside. Wash broccoli, divide into florets, taking care to keep a length of tender green stalk on each piece. If florets are large, slice with a sharp knife, cutting through stem as well. Pass the end of the stem through the slit in the prawn so that the floret rests within the curve of the prawn.

Heat wok, add oil and when oil is hot add ginger and prawns threaded with broccoli. stir-fry for 2 minutes. Add salt, water and wine, reduce heat to simmer, cover and cook for 3 minutes. Push prawns to side of wok, add cornflour mixed with water, stir until slightly thickened. Serve at once, garnished with shredded red chilli and accompanied by rice.

Stir-Fried Prawns with Oyster Sauce

Serves: 2

4	250 g (8 oz) raw prawns (shrimp)
0	2 tablespoons peanut oil
Tr	1 clove garlic, crushed
Tr	½ teaspoon finely grated fresh ginger
2	1 tablespoon oyster sauce
Tr	2 tablespoons Chinese wine or dry sherry
1	½ cup fish stock (page 156) or water
2.5	1 teaspoon cornflour (cornstarch)
0	1 tablespoon cold water
11	total grams carbohydrate

Shell and de-vein prawns. Heat oil. Fry garlic and ginger on low heat until soft and golden. Add prawns and stir-fry on medium heat until colour changes. Add sauce, wine or sherry, stock or water and bring to the boil. Cover and simmer 2 minutes, then stir in the cornflour mixed with the cold water and cook, stirring, until liquid thickens slightly and becomes clear. Serve at once with rice.

Note: Vegetables may be added to this dish. Stir-fry about 3 cups mixed vegetables or just one kind, cut into bite-sized pieces, after frying the ginger and garlic. Remove them from pan before adding prawns and return vegetables to pan to reheat after the sauce has been made. Vegetables and prawns must not be over-cooked.

Stir-Fried Shrimp with Bean Sprouts and Snow Peas *Serves: 4–6*

Tr	2 tablespoons dried wood fungus
4	250 g (8 oz) shrimp or small raw prawns
9	250 g (8 oz) fresh bean sprouts
12	12–18 snow peas (mange-tout)
4	2 celery stalks
0	2 tablespoons peanut oil
Tr	1 clove garlic, crushed
Tr	½ teaspoon finely grated fresh ginger
2.5	1 teaspoon cornflour (cornstarch)
4	1 teaspoon sugar
2	1 tablespoon light soy sauce
Tr	1 tablespoon Chinese wine or dry sherry
39.5	**total grams carbohydrate**

Soak wood fungus in hot water for 10 minutes. It will swell and soften. Trim off any gritty pieces. Shell and de-vein the prawns. Wash bean sprouts and drain. If tails are long and scraggly, pinch them off. Remove stems and strings from snow peas. Cut celery thinly in diagonal slices.

Heat oil in a wok. Add garlic and ginger and stir for 10 seconds, then add the sliced celery and stir-fry on high heat for 2 minutes. Add bean sprouts and fry for 1 minute longer or until vegetables are tender but still crisp. Remove from pan. Add very little more oil to wok and stir-fry the shrimp or prawns until they turn pink. Add snow peas and stir-fry for 30–40 seconds. Return vegetables and wood fungus, then move food to side of pan, thicken liquid slightly with the cornflour (cornstarch) mixed with the sugar, soy sauce and wine, and serve immediately.

Deep Fried Prawns with Chilli *Serves: 4*

8	500 g (1 lb) raw prawns (shrimp)
2.4	3 fresh red chillies
Tr	1 clove garlic
1	2 teaspoons finely grated fresh ginger
8	2 teaspoons sugar
0	oil for deep frying
2	1 tablespoon light soy sauce
Tr	1 tablespoon Chinese wine or dry sherry
22.4	**total grams carbohydrate**

Shell and de-vein the prawns, rinse and dry well on paper towels. Slit the chillies, remove and discard seeds, chop chillies finely. Crush garlic with a little of the measured sugar and mix with the chillies and ginger.

Heat about 1 cup of oil in a wok until very hot and deep fry the prawns a few at a time for 2 or 3 minutes or just until the colour changes. Do not fry too long. Remove from pan and drain on absorbent paper. Pour off most of oil from pan, leaving only about a tablespoon. Add the chilli, garlic and ginger mixture and fry on low heat, stirring. Add the remaining sugar, soy sauce and wine, then add prawns and stir only until reheated. Serve immediately with rice or noodles.

Stir-Fried Prawns in the Shell

Serves: 2–4

4	500 g (1 lb) medium-sized raw prawns (shrimp) in shell
0	3 tablespoons peanut oil
1	1 teaspoon finely grated fresh ginger
1	1 teaspoon finely chopped garlic
1	1 fresh red chilli, finely chopped, optional
1	2 tablespoons dry sherry
4	2 tablespoons light soy sauce
0	1 teaspoon sesame oil
8	2 teaspoons sugar
20	total grams carbohydrate

This is a wonderfully tasty dish to eat in a relaxed atmosphere. When I first tasted it, in Singapore, it was at one of those outdoor restaurants where the customers were serious about good food and used their hands to tackle the prawns.

Wash prawns and dry as well as possible on kitchen paper towels. Remove the long feelers but leave the shells intact.

Heat wok, add peanut oil and when very hot put in the prawns and stir-fry on high heat until they change colour. Add the ginger, garlic and chilli and fry for less than a minute, stirring constantly, then add all the remaining ingredients mixed together. Bring to the boil, stirring the prawns constantly in the sauce. Serve warm, or allow to cool to room temperature.

Stir-Fried Prawns in the Shell

Garlic Scallops

Serves: 4 as an appetiser

12	I dozen scallops on the shell
I	2 large cloves garlic
I	2 teaspoons light soy sauce
2	I tablespoon oyster sauce
Tr	I tablespoon dry sherry
2.5	I teaspoon cornflour (cornstarch)
0	I tablespoon cold water
0	2 tablespoons peanut oil
0	I teaspoon sesame oil
Tr	Mermaid's Tresses for garnish (optional, see below)
19	**total grams carbohydrate**

Remove scallops from shells. Wash and dry the shells. Dry the scallops thoroughly on paper towels. Finely chop the garlic. Mix together the soy sauce, oyster sauce and sherry. Mix cornflour with cold water in a separate container. Have all the ingredients assembled before starting to cook.

Heat a heavy frying pan and lightly grease it with peanut oil or olive oil spray. Sear scallops for 30 seconds each side and arrange them in the shells. Do not overcook scallops or they will shrink and toughen.

Add a little oil to the pan and on low heat fry the garlic for a few seconds, stirring. Do not let it brown or it will taste bitter. Pour in the mixed seasonings, cover and simmer for a further 2 minutes. Stir in the cornflour mixed with cold water and continue stirring until the sauce boils and thickens slightly. Add sesame oil and mix, then spoon over the scallops in their shells. Serve at once, garnished with Mermaid's Tresses if liked.

Mermaid's Tresses: The fanciful name given to finely sliced and crisply fried leaves of the dark green bok choy, so popular in many Chinese retaurants. Wipe over 4 leaves of bok choy with a barely damp kitchen paper towel to remove any sand, but don't wet them or they will splutter when fried. Roll the leaves tightly and, with a sharp knife, shred in very fine, even slices. Separate the shreds. Heat about a cup of oil in a wok until very hot and add a handful of the shredded leaves at a time. Fry on high heat for 60–80 seconds, then scoop them out on a perforated spoon and drain on paper towels. They should be bright green. In a few minutes when the leaves have cooled and become crisp to the touch, sprinkle with a pinch each of salt and caster sugar.

Garlic Scallops

Stir-Fried Scallops with Bamboo Shoots

Serves: 2–4

8	250 g (8 oz) scallop meat or whole scallops
3	8 dried Chinese mushrooms
5.2	½ cup bamboo shoots
12	125 g (4 oz) snow peas (12–16) (mange-tout)
0	2 tablespoons peanut oil
Tr	1 clove garlic, finely chopped
Tr	½ teaspoon finely grated fresh ginger
4	3 tablespoons chopped spring onions (scallions)
2	1 tablespoon light soy sauce
Tr	1 tablespoon dry sherry
0	1 teaspoon sesame oil
0	salt to taste

35.7	total grams carbohydrate

Drain scallop meat on paper towels. If scallop meat is not available, cut whole scallops in halves. Soak the mushrooms in hot water for 30 minutes, discard stems and slice the caps finely. Slice the bamboo shoots and quarter the slices. (Use winter bamboo shoots if possible.) String snow peas and leave them whole.

Heat peanut oil in a wok and fry garlic, ginger and spring onions on low heat until soft. Raise the heat and add the mushrooms and snow peas, stir-fry for 1 minute. Add scallops and bamboo shoots and stir-fry for 1 minute longer. Add soy sauce, sherry and sesame oil, cover and simmer for 1 minute. Add salt if necessary and serve at once.

Stir-Fried Scallops with Vegetables

Serves: 2–3

8	250 g (8 oz) scallops
2	2 sticks celery
12	125 g (4 oz) snow peas (mange-tout)
0	2 tablespoons peanut oil
Tr	½ teaspoon finely grated fresh ginger
2	1 tablespoon oyster sauce
1	2 teaspoons light soy sauce
0	salt to taste
25.5	**total grams carbohydrate**

This delicate dish must not be over-cooked so have seasonings measured in readiness for adding to pan and serve straight away.

Dry scallops on paper towels. Wash celery and cut in thin diagonal slices. Remove strings from snow peas.

Heat oil in wok or frying pan and fry the ginger for a minute over medium heat. Add scallops and fry on high heat, stirring, for 1 minute. Add snow peas and celery and toss for just 1 minute longer. Add oyster sauce and soy sauce and stir until well mixed. Sprinkle with salt and serve immediately.

Salt and Pepper Squid

Salt and Pepper Squid

Serves: 6

9	750 g (1½ lb) squid tubes
1	egg white
Tr	2 hot chillies, seeded and finely sliced
Tr	⅛ teaspoon Sichuan pepper or white pepper
Tr	1 clove garlic, crushed
0	½ teaspoon salt
0	2 cups peanut or light olive oil

DRY INGREDIENTS

24	3 tablespoons plain flour
20	3 tablespoons rice flour
16	1 tablespoon caster sugar
Tr	½ teaspoon white pepper

72	total grams carbohydrate

Cut the squid into rings, or strips if the rings are going to be very large. Whisk the egg white with chillies, garlic, pepper and salt and marinate squid for 1 hour at least.

Sift dry ingredients well to combine. Heat oil in wok to very hot. Just before frying, drain the squid and dust with the flour mixture, then shake in a sieve to get rid of excess flour. Deep fry in batches until lightly golden. It should take 1 minute or less. Drain on absorbent paper. Serve and eat hot.

Fried Squid, Sichuan Style

Serves: 4

6	500 g (1 lb) tender squid
0	½ teaspoon salt
0	1 tablespoon egg white
10	4 teaspoons cornflour (cornstarch)
0	1½ tablespoons peanut oil
3	1 small red capsicum (sweet pepper)
Tr	1 clove garlic
12	6 spring onions (scallions)
0	½ cup chicken stock (see page 156) or water
2	½ teaspoon each salt and sugar
0	1 teaspoon chilli oil
0	1 tablespoon cold water
0	1½ cups peanut oil
Tr	1 tablespoon preserved radish with chilli
34	**total grams carbohydrate**

Wash squid well. Discard head and inside of squid. Slit body of squid lengthways and cut into 5-cm x 2.5-cm (2-in x 1-in) pieces. Rinse well. On inner surface make diagonal slits with a sharp knife, first one way and then the other to give a pattern of small diamonds. Be careful not to cut right through. Combine squid with salt, egg white, 3 teaspoons cornflour and the peanut oil. Mix thoroughly and set aside while preparing other ingredients.

Remove seeds and membranes from capsicum and cut into thin strips. Chop the garlic finely and cut spring onions in bite-sized lengths. Have all ingredients prepared, measured and ready before starting to cook. Combine stock with salt, sugar and chilli oil. In a separate bowl mix remaining teaspoon cornflour with the cold water.

Heat the 1½ cups peanut oil in wok and when very hot add the squid and fry on high heat for just long enough to cook the squid, about 2 minutes. The squid curls as it cooks, showing the scoring on the inner surface. Do not over-cook or it will toughen. Pour contents of wok through wire frying spoon placed over a heatproof bowl.

Return wok to heat with just the oil that clings to the sides. Add the red capsicum, garlic, spring onion and radish and stir-fry over high heat for one minute. Return drained squid to wok.

Add stock mixture and as soon as the liquid comes to the boil stir in the cornflour mixture and stir until it thickens slightly. This should take only a few seconds. Serve immediately with ½ cup portions of rice.

Fried Chilli Crabs

3	2 medium-size raw crabs
0	½ cup peanut oil
2	2 teaspoons finely grated fresh ginger
1.5	3 cloves garlic, finely chopped
2.4	3 fresh red chillies, seeded and chopped
10.2	2 tablespoons tomato sauce
Tr	¼ cup Chinese chilli sauce
8	2 teaspoons sugar
2	1 tablespoon light soy sauce
0	1 teaspoon salt
29.1	total grams carbohydrate

Wash crabs well, scrubbing away any mossy patches on the shell. Remove hard top shell, stomach bag and fibrous tissue and with cleaver chop each crab into 4 pieces.

Heat a wok, add oil and when oil is very hot fry the crab pieces until they change colour, turning them so they cook on all sides. Remove to a plate.

Turn heat to low and fry the ginger, garlic and red chillies, stirring constantly, until they are cooked but not brown. Add the sauces, sugar, soy sauce and salt, bring to the boil, then return crabs to the wok and allow to simmer in the sauce for 3 minutes, adding very little water if sauce reduces too much. Serve with rice.

Braised Ginger Crab

3	2 mud crabs (dungeness) or 4 blue swimmer crabs
0	2 tablespoons peanut oil
Tr	1 clove garlic, finely chopped
Tr	1 tablespoon finely shredded fresh ginger
1	2 tablespoons light soy sauce
1	2 tablespoons dry sherry
0	¼ cup water
6	¼ cup finely sliced spring onions (scallions)
12	total grams carbohydrate

Wash crabs well, remove and discard hard top shell, fibrous tissue and stomach bag. If using mud crabs, separate the large claws and crack them. Divide each crab body in halves or quarters.

Heat the wok, add peanut oil and swirl, to spread the oil. On medium heat fry the garlic and ginger just until soft and starting to colour. Add the soy sauce, sherry, water and the crab, cover and simmer for 5–8 minutes. Sprinkle in the spring onions, replace cover and cook for 1 minute longer. Serve hot.

Note: If using raw crabs fry them on high heat until they change colour, then add ingredients and proceed as above.

Braised Ginger Crab

Lobster in Black Bean Sauce

Lobster in Black Bean Sauce

Serves: 4

2	2 fresh lobster tails, medium size
6	1½ tablespoons canned salted black beans
I	2 cloves garlic, crushed
4	I teaspoon sugar
0	4 tablespoons peanut oil
Tr	½ teaspoon garlic, finely chopped
I	I teaspoon fresh ginger, finely chopped
0	¾ cup hot water
2.5	I teaspoon cornflour (cornstarch)
0	I tablespoon cold water
3	2 tablespoons chopped spring onions (scallions)
Tr	I egg, slightly beaten
20.5	**total grams carbohydrate**

With a heavy cleaver, chop lobster tails into segments. Rinse black beans in a strainer under cold water for a few seconds, and drain. Mash beans well with crushed garlic and sugar. Heat oil in a wok and fry the chopped garlic and ginger until they start to brown, then add lobster segments, raise heat and stir-fry for 4–5 minutes, fuming them constantly. Remove cooked lobster tail from wok, add black bean mixture to the oil and fry for I minute. Replace the lobster pieces, add the hot water, stir well, cover wok and cook for 3 minutes. Stir in cornflour mixed with cold water, stir until sauce boils and thickens slightly, then add spring onions and egg and stir until egg sets. Serve at once with hot rice.

Note: If using cooked lobster it is not necessary to fry the lobster sections. Make the sauce first and simply heat the lobster in it before adding the cornflour, egg and spring onions.

Abalone with Chinese Cabbage

Serves: *2 as a main meal, 4 with other dishes*

2.3	half a 454 g (16 oz) can of abalone
4	1 Chinese cabbage (napa Cabbage)
Tr	1 tablespoon dry sherry
2	1 tablespoon oyster sauce
2	1 tablespoon light soy sauce
2	½ teaspoon sugar, optional
0	½ teaspoon sesame oil
0	1 tablespoon peanut oil
Tr	½ teaspoon finely grated fresh ginger
4	2 spring onions (scallions), cut into bite-sized pieces

17.3	total grams carbohydrate

Abalone is a luxury ingredient, so use half the can in another recipe.

Slice the abalone paper-thin and set aside. Wash the Chinese cabbage well and cut into bite-sized lengths, using all the stems and all but the tough portions of the leaves.

Combine the sherry, oyster sauce, soy sauce, sugar and sesame oil and have ready in a small bowl.

Heat a wok, add the peanut oil and swirl to coat. Add ginger and cabbage and stir-fry over high heat for 1 minute. Add all the seasonings and the spring onions. Lower heat, cover and simmer for 2 minutes, then stir in the abalone slices and heat gently only until abalone is warm. Do not over-cook or it will become tough. Serve immediately.

Abalone in Oyster Sauce

Serves: *4–5*

2.3	1 x 454 g (16 oz) can abalone
2	4 dried Chinese mushrooms
6	12 snow peas (mange-tout) or 4 leaves Chinese mustard cabbage
8	4 spring onions (scallions)

SAUCE

2	1 tablespoon oyster sauce
Tr	1 teaspoon soy sauce
Tr	1 tablespoon Chinese wine or brandy
0	¾ cup liquid from abalone
5	2 teaspoons cornflour (cornstarch)

26.3	total grams carbohydrate

Drain abalone, reserving liquid. Cut abalone into paper-thin slices. Soak mushrooms in hot water for 30 minutes, then cut off and discard stalks and slice each mushroom into 4. String snow peas (or cut mustard cabbage leaves into bite-sizedd pieces). Cut spring onions into similar lengths.

Sauce: Combine all liquid ingredients, add a little to the cornflour and mix until smooth, then combine with remaining liquid. Bring to the boil in a small pan, stirring constantly. Add mushrooms, snow peas (or cabbage) and spring onions. Cook, stirring, until the vegetables are tender but still crisp—about 2 or 3 minutes. Add abalone and just heat through. Do not cook abalone on high heat or for longer than is necessary to just heat it or it will toughen.

Serve with ½ cup portions of rice or noodles.

Poultry and Eggs

Chicken is a dieter's delight—a moderately priced, low fat, sustaining, high protein food. You can eat chicken to your heart's content in the carefully selected and adapted recipes in this chapter. Duck is permissible too, but go easy because though duck contains no carbohydrates it is a rich meat and needs a certain amount of starch to cushion and absorb the fat or you will feel uneasy after a meal. Since starches are limited on this diet, limit your intake of fatty meat too.

There are lots of recipes you can enjoy without the need for any starch accompaniment. For example, look at the recipe for Red Cooked Chicken (on page 95). That recipe may seem to contain a large number of carbohydrates but you will see that it is the soy sauce and sugar that contribute the largest number. These give flavour to the chicken but are not served with it— they form the 'master sauce', which is kept and used as a base for more 'red cooking'. The small amount of sauce that flavours the chicken adds hardly any carbohydrates so Red Cooked Chicken is a dish that should feature largely in your menus and will be ideal for cold lunches.

Chicken and Almonds

0	2 large chicken breasts
0	½ teaspoon salt
0	¼ teaspoon pepper
5	2 teaspoons cornflour (cornstarch)
0	½ teaspoon five spice powder
0	1 tablespoon peanut oil
Tr	1 tablespoon egg white
0	1½ cups peanut oil
5	2 tablespoons slivered almonds
4	1 cup halved straw mushrooms
1	½ cup chicken stock (see page 156)
Tr	1 teaspoon soy sauce
Tr	spring onion flowers or fresh coriander (cilantro) for garnish
16.5	**total grams carbohydrate**

You can enjoy this popular dish, but cheat a little by using slivered almonds in a reduced quantity to bring down the carbohydrate and calorie count.

Remove all skin from chicken breasts and bone the breasts with a sharp knife. Use skin and bones to make stock for this receipe. Cut chicken meat into dice, sprinkle with the salt and pepper, leave aside for 10 minutes. Sprinkle with cornflour, five spice powder and tablespoon of peanut oil and mix well. Set aside for a further 15 minutes, then add egg white and mix. Allow to marinate for 30 minutes.

Heat 1½ cups peanut oil in a wok and fry the slivered almonds until golden. Lift out on wire spoon and drain on absorbent paper. Drop marinated chicken into the hot oil in batches, separating it so it does not stick together. Fry for 1 minute or until colour changes. Do not over-cook. Lift out on slotted spoon as each batch is done, drain on absorbent paper. When all the chicken has been fried pour off all but 1 tablespoon of the oil.

Stir-fry the mushrooms until heated through, add stock and soy sauce. Return chicken to pan, heat to boiling, then remove from heat and serve, sprinkled with the fried almonds. Garnish dish with spring onion flowers or sprigs of fresh coriander.

Chicken with Chinese Cabbage

Serves: 2–4

0	2 large chicken breasts
0	½ teaspoon salt
0	¼ teaspoon pepper
Tr	1 tablespoon dry sherry
7.5	3 teaspoons cornflour (cornstarch)
0	1 tablespoon peanut oil
Tr	1 egg white
0	1½ cups peanut oil for deep frying
7.5	2 cups sliced Chinese cabbage (choy sum or gai choy)
Tr	½ teaspoon crushed garlic
Tr	½ teaspoon finely grated fresh ginger
2	1 tablespoon light soy sauce
2	1 tablespoon oyster sauce
21	**total grams carbohydrate**

Remove skin from chicken breasts. Bone the breasts with a sharp knife. (Use skin and bones for stock pot.) Cut the chicken meat into thin slices. Mix the salt and pepper into the dry sherry, sprinkle over the chicken meat and set aside for 10 minutes. Sprinkle with the cornflour and the tablespoon of peanut oil and mix well, set aside for a further 15 minutes, then add unbeaten egg white and mix thoroughly. Chill for 30 minutes.

Heat about 1½ cups peanut oil in a wok and fry the chicken in batches, separating the pieces as you drop them into the oil so they don't stick together. The oil should not be too hot. Fry for only half a minute, or just as long as it takes for the chicken to turn white. Immediately take out the pieces on a wire strainer or slotted spoon and drain. When they are all fried, pour most of the oil into a metal container for future use and return the wok to the heat with only about a tablespoon of oil in it.

Let the wok get hot again. Add the sliced cabbage, garlic and ginger and toss over high heat for 1 minute. Add the chicken, soy sauce and oyster sauce and stir-fry for a further minute, then turn heat low, cover and cook for 2 minutes. Serve immediately.

Chicken and Straw Mushrooms with Walnuts

Serves: 4

0	500 g (1 lb) chicken breasts
10	1 tablespoon cornflour (cornstarch)
0	1 teaspoon salt
0	½ teaspoon five spice powder
12	6 spring onions (scallions)
8	1 x 200 g (7 oz) can straw mushrooms
5.2	½ cup canned bamboo shoot
0	½ peanut oil for deep frying
4	¼ cup shelled walnuts
1	½ cup chicken stock (see page 156)
Tr	1 teaspoon light soy sauce
0	1 tablespoon cold water

40.7   total grams carbohydrate

Walnuts are comparatively low in carbohydrates. The ¼ cup used in this recipe only adds up to 4 grams, so don't feel guilty about enjoying a nice crunchy morsel. There won't be too many because the quantity is only a quarter of the amount in this non-diet version.

Skin and bone chicken breasts and simmer bones for stock. Cut chicken flesh into small dice. Combine 3 teaspoons of the cornflour, the salt and five spice powder and toss the chicken pieces in the flour mixture to coat lightly. Dust off excess. Cut spring onions into bite-sized lengths. Drain straw mushrooms and cut each in half lengthways. Dice the bamboo shoot.

Heat oil and deep fry the walnuts over medium heat, just for a minute. Do not let them brown or they will be bitter. Lift out on slotted spoon and drain on absorbent paper.

Fry the chicken pieces in two batches, over medium heat just until they change colour. This should take no longer than 1 minute for each batch. As they change colour, lift them out with slotted spoon and drain on absorbent paper.

Pour off all but 2 tablespoons oil. Add spring onions, mushrooms and bamboo shoot to pan and stir-fry over high heat for 1 minute. Add stock. Mix soy sauce and remaining teaspoon cornflour with 1 tablespoon cold water, add to pan and stir while bringing to the boil. As gravy thickens, add chicken pieces and heat through. Remove from heat, stir in walnuts and serve at once.

Chicken and Straw Mushrooms with Walnuts

Chicken with Vegetables in Oyster Sauce

Serves: 2–4

0	375 g (12 oz) chicken breast or thigh fillets
0	¼ teaspoon salt
0	⅛ teaspoon pepper
5	2 teaspoons cornflour (cornstarch)
0	3 tablespoons peanut oil
Tr	1 egg white
6	1 cup sliced cauliflower
Tr	½ teaspoon finely grated fresh ginger
Tr	1 small clove garlic, crushed
8	4 spring onions (scallions), cut into bite-sized pieces
4	1 red capsicum (sweet pepper), finely sliced
4	2 tablespoons oyster sauce

28.5   total grams carbohydrate

This recipe makes use of the Chinese technique of 'velveting', which is particularly useful when cooking meats that are inclined to be dry, such as chicken breast. The cornflour, peanut oil and egg white are added in stages, forming a protective coating over the meat. Velveted ingredients may be cooked in fast boiling water, as in this recipe, or deep-fried in oil.

Cut chicken into bite-sized pieces. Season with salt and pepper, leave for 10 minutes, then sprinkle with cornflour and 1 tablespoon peanut oil, mix well and set aside for 15 minutes. Add unbeaten egg white, mix well and chill for 30 minutes.

Bring a pan of lightly salted water to the boil with 1 tablespoon peanut oil, add the chicken and return to the boil, separating the pieces with chopsticks if they are inclined to stick together. Cook for 2 minutes then lift out the chicken with a wire strainer and drain.

Drop the slices of cauliflower into the same water and boil for 1 minute. Drain, and run cold water over the cauliflower to stop it cooking in its own heat.

Heat remaining tablespoon of oil in a wok and add the ginger, garlic, spring onions and capsicum. Stir-fry on high heat for 1 minute. Add oyster sauce, cauliflower and chicken pieces, stir and mix until heated through, then serve.

Chicken and Mushrooms in Lettuce Cups

Serves: 2–4

2	6 dried Chinese mushrooms
4	2 tablespoons dark soy sauce
8	2 teaspoons sugar
0	2 teaspoons sesame oil
0	2 tablespoons peanut oil
0	250 g (8 oz) chopped raw chicken thigh fillets
5.2	½ cup finely chopped bamboo shoot
2	½ cup finely chopped celery
9.5	4 water chestnuts, finely chopped
0	salt for seasoning, if necessary
3.6	12 lettuce leaves
2	1 tablespoon light soy sauce
Tr	2 tablespoons sherry
Tr	½ teaspoon finely grated ginger
2	1 teaspoon hoi sin sauce, optional

39.3	total grams carbohydrate

I was first served this dish in Hong Kong, and it was minced pigeon that was presented. Here is a more down-to-earth version, but delicious nonetheless. Serve as main dish for 2 or first course for 6.

Soak the mushrooms in hot water for 30 minutes. Discard stems. Cook the caps with ½ cup water, dark soy sauce, sugar and sesame oil for 10 minutes. Allow to cool and chop caps finely. Heat oil in a wok and stir-fry the chicken until cooked. Combine the chicken, chopped mushrooms and any liquid left in pan, bamboo shoot, celery and water chestnuts. Season to taste with salt if necessary. Serve savoury mixture with crisp lettuce leaves for making rolls. Combine light soy, sherry, ginger and hoi sin sauce and serve as a dip.

Chicken and Prawns with Broccoli

Serves: 4–6

0	1 whole chicken breast
0	½ teaspoon five spice powder
0	½ teaspoon salt
6	375 g (12 oz) shelled raw prawns (shrimp)
5	1 cup broccoli sprigs
0	2 tablespoons peanut oil
Tr	1 clove garlic, crushed
Tr	½ teaspoon finely grated fresh ginger
1	2 teaspoons light soy sauce
Tr	1 tablespoon Chinese wine or dry sherry
Tr	2 tablespoons chicken stock (page 156) or water
2.5	1 teaspoon arrowroot or cornflour (cornstarch)
0	2 teaspoons cold water
16.5	**total grams carbohydrate**

Bone chicken breast and remove the skin. Slice flesh thinly and mix with five spice powder and salt. De-vein prawns and if very large cut in halves. Mix with chicken and set aside.

Bring a little lightly salted water to the boil and drop in the broccoli sprigs. If there are any thick stems peel away the skin, cut into slices and drop into the water 1 minute before adding the florets. When water returns to the boil cover pot and simmer for 3 minutes, then drain and run cold water over the broccoli. This keeps the colour bright and prevents over-cooking.

Heat oil in a wok and add garlic and ginger. Stir-fry for 30 seconds, then add chicken and prawns and toss over high heat until chicken turns white and prawns turn pink. Add soy sauce, wine, stock or water and allow to simmer for 2 minutes. Mix arrowroot smoothly with cold water, add to liquid in pan and stir until it thickens. Add drained broccoli and toss gently to mix and heat through. Serve hot with rice.

Chicken Foo Yong

Serves: 2

0	1 small chicken breast (250g (8 oz) breast fillets)
0	2 tablespoons cold water
0	½ teaspoon salt
Tr	1 tablespoon dry sherry
Tr	4 egg whites
0	salt and pepper
2	1 tablespoon finely chopped spring onion (scallion), optional
0	2 tablespoons peanut oil
3	total grams carbohydrate

Skin and bone chicken breast. Chop chicken meat very finely until it is almost a paste, gradually work in the cold water to lighten the mixture, then mix in salt and sherry. Beat the egg whites until frothy, season with salt and pepper, add spring onion and fold into the chicken.

Heat peanut oil in a pan and pour in the egg white and chicken mixture, smoothing it to an even thickness. Cook until done on one side without allowing it to brown. Turn and cook on other side. Serve hot.

Braised Ginger Chicken

Serves: 4–6

0	1 x 1.5 kg (3 lb) chicken
3	1 piece tender fresh ginger
Tr	1 clove garlic
0	pinch salt
0	10 pieces Sichuan pepper or black peppercorns
0	2 tablespoons peanut oil
2	⅓ cup Chinese wine or dry sherry
12	2 teaspoons honey
6	¼ cup light soy sauce
0	1 segment star anise
23.5	total grams carbohydrate

Cut chicken into bite-sized serving pieces. Scrape brown skin off ginger and cut ginger into very thin slices, then into fine shreds until you have about ¼ cup. Crush the garlic with a sprinkling of salt. Heat the Sichuan pepper or peppercorns lightly in a dry pan, then crush with pestle or handle of Chinese chopper.

Heat wok, add oil and fry ginger and garlic over low heat just until pale golden. Add chicken pieces, raise heat to medium and fry until chicken changes colour. Add pepper, wine or sherry, honey, light soy sauce and star anise. Cover and simmer over low heat for 25 minutes, adding a little hot water toward end of cooking if necessary.

Braised Chicken with Mushrooms

Serves: 4

0	1 small roasting chicken or
	2 small chicken thighs
	per serving
1	2 tablespoons dry sherry
4	2 tablespoons light soy
1	1 teaspoon crushed garlic
1	1 teaspoon finely grated fresh ginger
0	½ teaspoon five spice powder
2	6 dried Chinese mushrooms or
	1 small can champignons
0	2 tablespoons peanut oil
1	½ cup hot stock or mushroom water
6	12 snow peas (mange-tout), optional
2.5	1 teaspoon cornflour (cornstarch)
18.5	**total grams carbohydrate**

A good, hearty winter dish. If liked, finish it in a casserole in the oven. For a low fat version of this recipe remove skin from chicken.

Joint chicken. Cut breast in quarters and if thighs are large, chop each in two. Combine sherry, soy, garlic, ginger and five spice powder and marinate the chicken in this mixture for 30 minutes. Meanwhile soak the dry mushrooms in hot water for 30 minutes, then discard stems and slice the caps.

Drain the pieces of chicken, reserving the marinade. Heat a wok or flameproof casserole and pour in the oil. Swirl wok to coat surface with oil. Brown the chicken over high heat, turning the pieces so that all surfaces come in contact with the heat. Add the reserved marinade and stock or water mushrooms soaked in. Add sliced mushrooms or champignons. Bring to the boil, then lower heat, cover and simmer for 25–30 minutes. Or transfer everything to a casserole or sandy pot and cook in a moderate oven for 45 minutes.

Bring a little lightly salted water to the boil and cook the snow peas for 1 minute. Drain immediately and refresh under cold water. Combine cornflour with a tablespoon of cold water, stir into juices in pan and allow to boil and thicken. Transfer to serving dish or serve in the casserole. Garnish with the snow peas and serve with a small portion of rice.

Note: If snow peas are not available, substitute ½ cup sliced celery cooked in the same way. This will reduce the carbohydrate count by 4 grams.

Braised Honey Chicken

Serves: 4–6

0	1 x 1.5 kg (3 lb) roasting chicken
0	2 tablespoons peanut oil
6	¼ cup dark soy sauce
12	2 teaspoons honey
0	1 whole star anise
1	3 tablespoons dry sherry
Tr	½ teaspoon crushed garlic
Tr	½ teaspoon finely grated fresh ginger
0	¼ cup stock or water if necessary
0	fresh coriander (cilantro) or spring onion (scallion) for garnish
20	**total grams carbohydrate**

The non-diet version of this recipe uses four times as much honey, but even with the modified amount it is delicious because of the extra added flavours such as star anise and ginger.

Cut chicken into joints and dry them well on paper towels. Heat the peanut oil in a wok and brown the chicken, a few pieces at a time, on high heat. Remove from wok as they are browned and repeat until all are done. Pour off excess oil, leaving only about a tablespoon. Return chicken, add soy sauce, honey, star anise, sherry, garlic and ginger. Stir well and turn the chicken joints in the mixture. Lower heat, cover and cook for 35–40 minutes or until chicken is tender. If necessary, add a little stock or water as liquid reduces. Serve garnished with sprigs of fresh coriander or spring onion curls.

Steamed Chicken and Lap Cheong with Vegetables

Serves: 2

0	1 large chicken breast
Tr	1 tablespoon dry sherry
2	1 tablespoon light soy sauce
2	1 pair lap cheong (Chinese sausages)
4	2 spring onions (scallions), sliced
7	1 cup broccoli sprigs
6	60 g (2 oz) snow peas
9.5	4 water chestnuts, sliced
31	**total grams carbohydrate**

Remove skin and bone from chicken breast and cut the meat into bite-sized slices. Marinate chicken in sherry and soy sauce in a heatproof dish. Add lap cheong and vegetables. Place dish in a steamer and steam over boiling water for 15–20 minutes or until chicken and lap cheong are soft and vegetables are just tender. Cut lap cheong into very thin diagonal slices and serve at once.

Braised Chicken with Lily Buds and Mushrooms

Serves: 4–6

0	1 x 1.5 kg (3 lb) chicken
4	2 tablespoons soy sauce
1	1 teaspoon finely grated fresh ginger
Tr	½ teaspoon crushed garlic
0	½ teaspoon salt
6	20 dried lily buds (golden needles)
2	6 dried Chinese mushrooms
Tr	1 tablespoon dried wood fungus
4	4 ears canned or fresh baby corn, cut in halves
0	2 tablespoons peanut oil
0	¾ cup stock
2	1 tablespoon fine shreds of fresh ginger
2.5	1 teaspoon cornflour (cornstarch)
0	2 teaspoons cold water

22.5	total grams carbohydrate

Cut chicken into pieces and rub over with a mixture of the soy sauce, ginger, garlic and salt. Set aside.

Soak lily buds, mushrooms and wood fungus separately in hot water for 30 minutes. Pinch hard ends off lily buds and cut them in halves, crosswise, or tie a knot in each, then pinch off hard ends. Discard mushroom stems and cut away any gritty parts.

Heat a wok, add the peanut oil and swirl wok to coat with oil, then add the chicken and brown quickly on all sides. Add the stock and ginger, lily buds and mushrooms, turn heat low, cover and braise for 25 minutes. Add wood fungus and heat through. Stir in cornflour mixed with the cold water and let it come to the boil and thicken slightly. Serve hot.

Braised Chicken with Lily Buds and Mushrooms

Steamed Chicken with Mushrooms and Ham

Serves: 2

0	half a small roasting chicken
Tr	2 tablespoons dry sherry
2	1 tablespoon light soy sauce
Tr	1 clove garlic, crushed
0	1 teaspoon sesame oil
2	6 dried Chinese mushrooms
0	½ cup thin strips of cooked ham
5	total grams carbohydrate

Wash the chicken and dry on paper towels. Marinate in the sherry, soy sauce, garlic and sesame oil for 1 hour. Meanwhile, soak mushrooms in hot water for 30 minutes, discard stems and cut caps into thin shreds.

Put chicken and marinade in a heatproof dish, scatter mushrooms and ham over, cover and steam for 30–35 minutes until chicken is tender. Cut into bite-sized pieces and serve hot or cold.

Steamed Chicken with Ginger

Serves: 2

0	half a small roasting chicken
Tr	2 tablespoons dry sherry
4	2 tablespoons light soy sauce
2	2 tablespoons fine shreds of fresh ginger
12	6 spring onions (scallions), cut into bite-sized pieces
18.5	total grams carbohydrate

Wash the chicken and dry it on paper towels. Marinate in the sherry, soy sauce, ginger and spring onion for at least 1 hour in a heatproof dish. Place the dish in a steamer or on a rack over boiling water in a wok. Cover and steam for 30–35 minutes, until chicken is tender. Chop into bite-sized pieces and serve.

Chicken in Black Bean Sauce

Serves: 2

0	1 large chicken breast
6	1 cup bean sprouts or 3 stalks celery
1	2 teaspoons canned salted black beans
Tr	1 teaspoon soy sauce
Tr	1 clove garlic, crushed
Tr	1 tablespoon sherry
0	½ cup cold stock or water
2.5	1 teaspoon cornflour (cornstarch)
0	1 tablespoon oil
11	**total grams carbohydrate**

Cut chicken meat off the bone, saving the bone for stock, then dice the meat. Wash and pick over the bean sprouts, discarding any brown ones. Leave to drain. (Cut celery in thin diagonal slices.) Put the black beans in a bowl and mash with a fork. Combine with soy sauce, garlic, sherry and half the liquid. Mix the cornflour into the remaining liquid.

Heat oil in a wok, add chicken and fry, stirring, for 2 minutes. Add the black bean mixture and stir until it boils. Add cornflour mixture and stir constantly until it boils and thickens, about 1 minute. Add the bean sprouts (or celery slices) and toss in the sauce for 1 minute longer. Serve at once with rice.

Drunken Chicken

Serves: 2–4

0	1 x 1 kg (2 lb) roasting chicken
3	¾ cup dry sherry
0	½ teaspoon salt
1	1 tablespoon finely shredded fresh ginger
2	1 spring onion (scallion), sliced
6	**total grams carbohydrate**

Cut chicken in halves lengthways, wash well and dry on paper towels. Combine the sherry, salt, ginger and spring onion in a large dish and marinate the chicken in this mixture for 2 hours or longer.

Put chicken and marinade into a large pot, add enough water to just cover chicken, bring to the boil and simmer very gently, covered with a well fitting lid, for 20 minutes. turn off heat and allow chicken to cool in the liquid. Cut into bite-sized pieces and serve at room temperature with a dip of light soy sauce mixed with the strained stock, about 1 tablespoon soy to 3 of stock.

Note: For a stronger flavour, marinate the cooked chicken in extra sherry overnight.

Fried Chicken, Sichuan-Style

Serves: 6

0	500 g (1 lb) chicken breasts
5	2 teaspoons cornflour (cornstarch)
0	1 teaspoon salt
0	½ teaspoon five spice powder
0	1 tablespoon egg white
0	1 tablespoon peanut oil
1	½ cup chicken stock (see page 156)
8	2 teaspoons sugar
2	1 tablespoon light soy sauce
0	½ teaspoon sesame oil
Tr	1 teaspoon vinegar
Tr	2 teaspoons Chinese wine or dry sherry
0	¼ teaspoon Sichuan pepper, optional
2.5	1 teaspoon cornflour (cornstarch)
0	1 tablespoon cold water
0	½ cup peanut oil for frying
Tr	5 dried red chillies, seeded
1	2 cloves garlic, finely chopped
1	2 teaspoons finely chopped fresh ginger
8	4 spring onions (scallions), chopped in 5cm (2-in) lengths
30	**total grams carbohydrate**

Bone chicken breasts and cut meat into bite-sized pieces. Mix together 2 teaspoons cornflour, salt and ½ teaspoon five spice powder and toss chicken pieces in the mixture to coat. Shake in a sieve to get rid of excess cornflour. Add egg white and peanut oil and mix with the hand to give the chicken a coating which will prevent it from becoming dry when cooked.

In a small bowl, mix together the chicken stock, sugar, soy sauce, sesame oil, vinegar, wine and pepper. In another small bowl combine the remaining teaspoon of cornflour and tablespoon of cold water.

Heat ½ cup peanut oil in a wok and when very hot add chicken pieces, a third at a time, and fry on high heat, tossing chicken to brown all over. As each batch is fried drain on paper towels and let oil return to high heat before adding next batch. When all the chicken has been fried, pour off oil leaving about 2 tablespoons in the wok. Add chillies, garlic and ginger and fry until garlic and ginger are golden and chillies turn dark. Add spring onions and toss for a few seconds, then add stock mixture and bring to the boil. Stir the small amount of cornflour and cold water again to mix smoothly and add to the pan, stirring constantly until it boils and thickens. Add chicken and toss to heat through. Serve at once with steamed rice.

Red Cooked Chicken

0	1 x 1.75 kg (3½ lb) chicken, whole
0	1½ cups cold water
15	1½ cups dark soy sauce
2	¼ cup Chinese wine or dry sherry
2	5-cm (2-in) piece fresh ginger, peeled and sliced
Tr	1 clove garlic
0	2 whole star anise
16	1 tablespoon sugar
0	2 teaspoons sesame oil
35.5	**total grams carbohydrate**

Red cooking is the term applied to cooking in soy sauce. The liquid that remains after cooking is called a master sauce and may be frozen for future use. Although the total number of carbohydrate grams is high, the largest percentage is in the sauce and very little sauce is served with the chicken.

Wash chicken well and leave to drain while preparing other ingredients. Choose a saucepan into which the chicken will just fit so that the soy liquid covers as much of the bird as possible. Put chicken into saucepan, breast down, then add all the ingredients except sesame oil. Bring slowly to the boil, then lower heat, cover and simmer very gently for 15 minutes. With tongs, turn chicken over, replace lid and simmer 20 minutes, basting breast with soy mixture every 5 minutes.

Remove from heat, leave covered in the saucepan until cool. Lift chicken out of sauce, place on serving platter and brush with sesame oil. This gives the chicken a glistening appearance as well as extra flavour.

Traditionally the chicken is placed on a chopping board and cut into two lengthways with a sharp cleaver. Each half is chopped into 3.5-cm (1½-in) strips and reassembled in the original shape. If this proves too much of an undertaking simply carve the chicken into joints. Serve at room temperature with a little of the cooking liquid as a dipping sauce.

Stir-Fried Chicken and Ham

Serves: 2–4

0	1 large chicken breast
5	2 teaspoons cornflour (cornstarch)
0	¼ teaspoon salt
0	3 tablespoons peanut oil
Tr	half an egg white
0	1 ham steak, 1 cm (¼ in) thick
4	1 cup sliced celery
9	1 medium onion
Tr	½ teaspoon grated fresh ginger
Tr	½ teaspoon crushed garlic
1	2 teaspoons oyster sauce or light soy sauce
20.5	**total grams carbohydrate**

Skin and bone the chicken breast. Cut the meat into bite-sized pieces and roll them in the cornflour and salt mixed together. Pour 1 tablespoon oil over and mix well by hand. Set aside for 10 minutes, then add the unbeaten egg white and mix again by hand so all the pieces are well coated. Chill for 20–30 minutes.

Cut ham into thin strips about 5-cm (2-in) long. Slice the celery in thin crescent shapes and measure the required amount. Wedge-cut the onion. To do this, cut the onion in halves lengthways, lay the halves cut side down on the chopping board and cut each one into 2 lengthwise sections. Cut these in halves crossways. Thus you get 8 sections from half an onion. Now separate the layers of onion so that there are bite-sized pieces which take only a few seconds to cook.

Heat a wok until very hot, add remaining two tablespoons of oil and swirl to coat wok. Add ginger and garlic, stir briefly, add ham strips and celery slices and toss over high heat for 1 minute. Move ham and celery to side of wok and let the oil run to the centre.

Add the chicken to the oil and turn the pieces over until all the chicken has turned white. Now add the onions and stir-fry the entire contents of the pan, for 1 minute. Add the oyster sauce or soy sauce, mix thoroughly and serve at once, garnished with spring onion curls or carrot flowers.

Crystal Cooked Chicken

Serves: 6

0	1 x 1.75 kg (3½ lb) roasting chicken
3	chicken stock (see page 156) or water
1	¼ cup sherry
2	6 slices fresh ginger
4	2 spring onions (scallions)
Tr	few celery leaves
0	1 teaspoon salt

10.5   total grams carbohydrate

Wash chicken well inside and out, then dry well on paper towels. Choose a pot just large enough to hold the chicken. Heat the stock or water, sherry, ginger, spring onions, celery leaves and salt to boiling. Gently lower in the chicken and if it is not quite immersed in liquid, add more boiling water until liquid covers chicken. Bring back to the boil, then turn heat as low as possible, cover and simmer for 20–25 minutes. Remove from heat and without removing lid let chicken finish cooking in the stored heat for 1 hour.

Have ready a large bowl of iced water with plenty of ice cubes in it. Lift the chicken from the pot, allowing any liquid inside the cavity to drain into the pot, and plunge the bird into the cold water. Leave to chill for 15 minutes, immersed in the ice water, then drain well, put into a dish and refrigerate overnight or at least 4 hours. This method of quick chilling results in a layer of delicious jellied stock between skin and flesh. Keep covered and chilled until serving time.

The chicken may be sliced and served cold, accompanied by dipping sauces, if liked. The water it was cooked in makes an excellent base for soup.

Stir-Fried Chicken and Asparagus

Serves: 2

0	250 g (8 oz) chicken breast meat (1 large chicken breast)
1	2 teaspoons light soy sauce
Tr	½ teaspoon crushed garlic
8	12 fresh green asparagus spears
2	half a medium-sized red capsicum (sweet pepper)
4.5	half a medium-sized onion
1	2 teaspoons oyster sauce
Tr	2 teaspoons dry sherry
Tr	2 tablespoons water or stock
0	2 tablespoons peanut oil
18	**total grams carbohydrate**

A dish as colourful as it is delicious, the brilliant green asparagus and bright red capsicum contrasting with the white meat of the chicken. When fresh asparagus is out of season, you can substitute 1 cup sliced broccoli or ½ cup thinly sliced green beans without upsetting the carbohydrate content.

Remove skin and bones (reserve for the stock pot) and cut the chicken meat into thin slices. Cut the slices into bite-sized pieces. Stir together the light soy sauce and crushed garlic in a bowl, add the chicken and mix well by hand so that all the chicken is flavoured.

Wash the asparagus thoroughly and if the ends of the stalks are tough, trim them. Thinly peel the bottom ends of the stalks for at least 2 cm (1 in). Slice asparagus stalks diagonally. Keep tips whole. Cut capsicum into strips. Wedge-cut the onion by cutting into four lengthways and cutting each piece across. Divide into layers. In a small bowl combine the oyster sauce, sherry and water.

Heat a wok, add 1 tablespoon of peanut oil and swirl to coat the wok. Add the marinated chicken and stir-fry on high heat for 1 minute or until all the chicken has changed colour. Remove to a plate. There should be enough oil left in the wok to stir-fry the capsicum and onion, but if necessary add about a teaspoonful. Fry capsicum and onion for 1 minute, remove to plate. Add remaining oil to wok and stir-fry the asparagus on high heat for 1 minute, turn heat low, add combined liquid ingredients, cover and simmer for 3 minutes by which time the asparagus will be tender but still crisp. Return chicken and other vegetables and stir just until heated through. Serve at once.

Stir-Fried Chicken and Asparagus

Roasted Spiced Chicken

Serves: 6

0	1 x 1.5 kg (3 lb) roasting chicken
6	¼ cup soy sauce
0	2 tablespoons peanut oil
1	2 tablespoons dry sherry
Tr	½ teaspoon crushed garlic
Tr	½ teaspoon finely grated fresh ginger
0	2 teaspoons five spice powder
8	1 tablespoon hoi sin sauce
0	¼ teaspoon ground black pepper
16	total grams carbohydrate

Wash chicken and dry on paper towels. Mix together the remaining ingredients and rub it well all over the chicken. Spoon some of the marinade into the cavity also. Cover and marinate in refrigerator overnight, or at room temperature at least 1 hour.

Preheat oven to 180°C (350°F). Place chicken in an oiled roasting pan and roast in a moderate oven for 1 hour 20 minutes, basting or brushing every 20 minutes with the marinade. Turn the chicken first on one side, then on the other and finish cooking breast upwards.

This chicken may be served warm or at room temperature. To carve Chinese style, place chicken on a chopping board and cut into two lengthways with a sharp cleaver. Then place each half cut side downwards and chop into strips, reassembling them on the serving platter. Alternatively, carve the chicken into joints.

Note: If preferred, prepare this dish with chicken drumsticks or wings instead of a whole chicken. Cooking time will be 45 minutes to 1 hour. Arrange marinated chicken in roasting pan in one layer and turn pieces half-way through cooking.

Smoked Tangerine Chicken

0	1 x 1.5 kg (3 lb) roasting chicken
2	1 tablespoon light soy sauce
0	1 teaspoon salt
4	1 teaspoon sugar
Tr	1 tablespoon Chinese wine or dry sherry
Tr	1 piece dried tangerine peel about the size of a rose leaf
0	1 whole star anise
0	3 tablespoons brown sugar
0	fresh coriander (cilantro) leaves to garnish
7	**total grams carbohydrate**

Wipe chicken inside and out with paper towels. Combine soy sauce, salt, sugar and wine and rub inside and outside the chicken. Marinate for 20 minutes, then put in a steamer and steam for 15 minutes.

In a mortar and pestle crush the tangerine peel and star anise as finely as possible and mix with brown sugar. Take a stout saucepan with a well-fitting lid, large enough to hold the whole chicken. Line the base of the pan with heavy-duty foil, bringing it a little way up the side of the pan. Sprinkle sugar and spice mixture evenly over foil, then put a trivet or wire rack in pan and put chicken on it. Cover pan tightly, put over medium heat and when smoke starts escaping under lid turn heat very low and smoke chicken for 15 minutes or until done.

This chicken dish can be served hot, at room temperature or cold. Slice the flesh off the bones and arrange on a platter, or chop through bones into small serving pieces. Garnish with sprigs of coriander.

Note: The brown sugar is used for smoke only and does not add to carbohydrate content.

Barbecue-Style Roast Duck

Serves: 4

0	1 x1.75 kg (3½ lb) roasting duck
Tr	1 clove garlic, crushed
1	1 teaspoon finely grated fresh ginger
2	1 teaspoon hoi sin sauce
1	1 teaspoon sesame paste
24	1 tablespoon honey
2	1 tablespoon soy sauce
0	1 teaspoon salt
0	½ teaspoon pepper
30.5	**total grams carbohydrate**

Preheat oven to 180–190°C (350–375°F). Wash duck inside and out, remove neck and giblets and reserve for making stock. Combine all other ingredients in a small saucepan and heat gently until honey melts and all ingredients are smoothly incorporated. Simmer for 2 minutes, adding a spoonful of water if it seems too thick.

Rub marinade all over duck, inside and out. Reserve remaining marinade to serve as a sauce with the duck. Put duck into oven bag or wrap in foil. If using oven bag, follow manufacturer's instructions and do not fail to make 3 or 4 holes in top of bag near the tie.

Place duck breast side downwards in roasting pan and cook in a moderate oven for 45 minutes. Turn duck breast side up and cook a further 45 minutes to 1 hour. Remove from bag, carve duck and serve hot with reserved marinade, spring onions and cucumber cut into matchstick strips. Serve with ½ cup portions of rice.

Barbecue-Style Roast Duck

Stir-Fried Chicken Livers

Serves: 2–4

7	250 g (8 oz) chicken livers
0	½ teaspoon salt
0	¼ teaspoon five spice powder
Tr	1 tablespoon dry sherry
2	1 tablespoon light soy sauce
Tr	¼ cup chicken stock (see page 156)
2	½ teaspoon sugar, optional
Tr	2 tablespoons peanut oil
Tr	1 clove garlic, crushed
5.2	½ cup sliced bamboo shoot
4	1 red or green capsicum (sweet pepper), sliced
1.2	½ teaspoon cornflour (cornstarch)
0	2 teaspoons cold water
4	2 spring onions (scallions), finely sliced
27.4	total grams carbohydrate

Wash the chicken livers, drain well and with a sharp knife remove tubes and any yellow spots. Cut into slices. Sprinkle with salt, five spice and sherry and set aside. In a small cup combine the soy sauce, stock and sugar.

Heat peanut oil in a wok, swirl to coat wok with oil, add the crushed garlic and cook over low heat, stirring, for a few seconds. Raise heat, add the bamboo shoot and capsicum and stir-fry for 1 minute. Add chicken livers and stir-fry for 1 minute. Add combined stock and bring to the boil, then stir in cornflour mixed smoothly with cold water and stir constantly until liquid boils and thickens slightly. Stir in spring onions and serve hot.

Chicken Livers with Mushrooms

7	250 g (8 oz) chicken livers
0	salt and pepper
2.5	8 dried Chinese mushrooms
2	1 tablespoon dark soy sauce
0	1 teaspoon sesame oil
4	1 teaspoon sugar
6	1 cup fresh bean sprouts
8	4 spring onions (scallions)
0	¼ cup chicken stock (see page 156) or water
2	1 tablespoon light soy
Tr	1 tablespoon dry sherry
0	2 tablespoons peanut oil
Tr	1 teaspoon crushed garlic
Tr	1 teaspoon finely grated fresh ginger
6	3 cups finely shredded Chinese cabbage
1.2	½ teaspoon cornflour (cornstarch)
0	2 teaspoons cold water

40.2   total grams carbohydrate

Served on a bed of stir-fried Chinese cabbage (the pale green, closely packed leafy kind called napa cabbage or wongah bak), this simple dish is a main course for 2 or part of a selection for 4.

Wash and drain chicken livers. Cut into bite-sized pieces, discarding any tubes or yellow spots. Sprinkle with salt and pepper and set aside. Soak mushrooms in hot water for 20 minutes, drain (saving ½ cup water), discard stems and cut caps into very thin slices. Put the slices into a small saucepan with the dark soy sauce, sesame oil and sugar and ½ cup of mushroom water. Simmer for 10 minutes or until almost all the liquid is absorbed. Set aside.

Wash bean sprouts and pick off any straggly brown tails. Cut spring onions into bite size lengths. Combine stock or water with light soy sauce and sherry. Set aside.

Heat a wok, add 1 tablespoon of peanut oil and swirl to coat inside of wok. Add half each of the garlic and ginger and give a quick stir, then add the shredded cabbage and toss over high heat for 1 minute. Remove from wok, arrange on a serving plate.

Add remaining tablespoon peanut oil to wok, fry remaining garlic and ginger on low heat for a few seconds, then turn heat high, add the chicken liver pieces and stir-fry until they lose their pinkness. Add the mushrooms, bean sprouts and spring onions and continue to stir-fry for a minute longer. Pour in the stock, soy sauce and sherry mixture and bring to the boil, cover and simmer for 1 minute. Stir in cornflour mixed smoothly with cold water and let it boil and thicken slightly. Spoon over the bed of stir-fried cabbage and serve at once.

Note: Shredded silverbeet or spinach may be substituted for Chinese cabbage.

POULTRY AND EGGS ■ 105

Braised Duck with Lily Buds

Serves: 3–4

0	1.5 kg (3 lb) roasting duck
Tr	1 teaspoon finely grated fresh ginger
0	½ teaspoon salt
0	¼ teaspoon pepper
1	1 teaspoon hoi sin sauce
Tr	2 teaspoons soy sauce
3	8 dried Chinese mushrooms
3	20 dried lily buds (golden needles)
0	2 tablespoons peanut oil
1	½ cup stock
2.5	1 teaspoon cornflour (cornstarch)
0	1 tablespoon cold water
12.5	**total grams carbohydrate**

Remove giblets and neck from inside duck and keep for making stock. With a heavy cleaver split duck in half lengthways. Wash and dry well with paper towels.

Combine ginger, salt, pepper, hoi sin sauce and 1 teaspoon of the soy sauce. Rub well all over duck. Soak mushrooms and lily buds in hot water for 20 minutes. Cut off mushroom stems and discard. Squeeze excess water from caps. Cut lily buds in halves crossways. (It is quicker if you lay them in a neat bundle and cut them all at once.)

Heat oil in a wok or heavy frying pan. With a knife scrape as much marinade as possible off duck and reserve. Brown duck on both sides. (If using a flat frying pan a little more oil will be necessary, but after browning duck pour off all but 2 tablespoons.) Add mushrooms and lily buds and fry for a minute or two longer. Add ¾ cup of the water mushrooms have soaked in, mixed with the reserved marinade. Cover pan, lower heat and simmer 15 minutes. Turn duck over, simmer 20 minutes longer or until duck is tender. Turn off heat. Place duck on board and with a sharp chopper separate wings, legs and thighs. Chop remaining pieces into 3.5-cm (1½-in) slices. Arrange on dish with mushrooms and lily buds.

Spoon off as much fat as possible from pan, then add stock and remaining soy sauce. Bring to the boil. Stir in cornflour mixed smoothly with cold water and continue stirring until sauce boils and thickens. Pour over duck and serve immediately with boiled rice.

Eggs Foo Yong with Barbecued Pork

Serves: 2–4

2	4 eggs
0	¼ teaspoon salt
0	⅛ teaspoon pepper
0	peanut oil
Tr	1 clove garlic, finely grated
Tr	½ teaspoon finely grated fresh ginger
8	4 spring onions (scallions), finely chopped
1	½ cup finely chopped barbecued pork
12	total grams carbohydrate

Beat eggs with salt and pepper, set aside. Heat 1 tablespoon oil in wok over medium heat and fry the garlic, ginger and spring onions until soft. Add pork and toss for 1 minute. Remove from wok and mix into the beaten egg. Wipe out the wok, heat a little oil and fry ¼ cup of the mixture at a time. If preferred, it may be fried as one large omelette, turning and browning the second side when the first side is cooked.

Steamed Omelettes

Serves: 2

2	4 eggs
0	¼ teaspoon salt
0	⅛ teaspoon pepper
2	125 g (4 oz) shelled prawns (shrimp)
2	1 spring onion (scallion), finely chopped
1	2 teaspoons light soy sauce
Tr	¼ teaspoon finely grated fresh ginger
0	1 teaspoon peanut oil

SAUCE

4	2 tablespoons oyster sauce
0	⅓ cup water
1.2	½ teaspoon cornflour (cornstarch)
0	2 teaspoons cold water
0	chilli sauce, optional

12.7	**total grams carbohydrate**

These are made in the form of little pouches with a filling of prawns or pork, and served with oyster sauce or sweet-sour sauce.

Beat eggs with salt and pepper. De-vein prawns, chop and mix with the spring onion, light soy sauce and grated ginger. Heat a wok, add a teaspoon of peanut oil and swirl to coat wok, then pour in a little of the beaten egg to form a small omelette about 10 cm (4 in) across. Put a teaspoonful of the prawn mixture in the centre, fold over and gently press edges of omelette together. Lift out onto a heatproof plate. When all the omelettes are made, place on steaming rack over gently boiling water in a wok. Cover and steam for 10–15 minutes and serve hot with sauce.

Sauce: In a small saucepan heat the oyster sauce and water, mix the cornflour with 2 teaspoons cold water and stir in, allow to boil and thicken slightly. If liked, stir in a very little chilli sauce.

Meat

In this chapter are recipes for many kinds of meat—beef, pork, lamb (yes, lamb is used in Northern China) and even veal. Although veal is not available in a country where cattle are valuable working animals, it is too easy to cook, too tasty and too suitable for a weight loss diet to leave out of this book.

Perhaps you will wonder why there is no recipe for Sweet and Sour Pork, one of the stalwarts of Chinese restaurants. I will tell you why. One hearty serving of this dish with its batter coating around the pork and its heavily sweetened sauce and you can upset the workings of your low carbohydrate eating plan!

Another point to keep in mind is that although pork, even fatty pork, contains no carbohydrate it is a rich meat that will give you a feeling of discomfort if eaten too freely, especially without the large amount of rice or noodles needed to absorb the richness.

I urge you to choose with care when eating at a restaurant and if certain restaurants favour heavily thickened sauces, eat just enough of the sauce to flavour the meat, send back the rest.

Though I have indicated the ideal cuts of meat to use, any cheaper cuts may be used for dishes requiring long cooking. However, when it comes to the short-cooked, stir-fried dishes so prominent in Chinese cuisine the best cuts for the best results are beef fillet, rump or Scotch fillet, pork fillet, chump or loin. These cuts are not cheap, but remember that in Chinese cooking meat goes a long way and feeds many more people than it could when served as a steak or chops. When you're in a hurry you have to buy tender (and more expensive) cuts of meat, but when there is time for marination you can use more economical cuts.

This is the Chinese method of marination. First, cut the meat in paper-thin slices or strips. It is easier to do this if the meat is partially frozen, making it firmer to handle. Trim the meat so that when it is sliced it will be in bite-sized pieces, small enough not to require further cutting since knives are never part of the table setting.

Lean steak such as round or blade or fresh silverside may be used for stir-fried dishes instead of fillet and rump. You may slice and marinate more than you need for one meal, and use it over a period of 3 or 4 days. To each 500 g (1 lb) of meat dissolve ½ teaspoon bicarbonate of soda (baking soda) in 3 tablespoons warm water. Add to meat with salt and other seasonings and knead well until meat absorbs liquid. Cover and refrigerate for at least 2 hours, preferably longer—overnight if possible. Proceed with the recipe in the usual way. This method is used in many Chinese restaurants, making economy cuts as tender as the choicest fillet.

Beef with Bamboo Shoot

Serves: 3–4

0	375 g (12 oz) fillet or rump steak (tenderloin or sirloin)
2	1 tablespoon soy sauce
0	½ teaspoon salt
Tr	1 clove garlic, crushed
Tr	½ teaspoon finely grated fresh ginger
0	¼ teaspoon five spice powder
0	2 tablespoons peanut oil
1	½ cup stock or water
5	2 teaspoons cornflour (cornstarch)
0	2 tablespoons cold water
10.4	1 cup sliced bamboo shoot
19.4	**total grams carbohydrate**

Cut meat into paper-thin slices, sprinkle soy sauce, salt, garlic, ginger and five spice powder over, and mix well by hand to season all the pieces of beef.

Heat oil in a wok or large frying pan and when very hot add the beef and toss over high heat until colour changes. Add stock, stir in cornflour mixed with cold water and boil, stirring, until gravy becomes thick and clear. Add sliced bamboo shoot and heat through.

Steamed Beef with Snow Peas

Serves: 2–4

0	375 g (12 oz) lean steak
Tr	½ teaspoon finely grated fresh ginger
Tr	2 teaspoons bean sauce (min sze jeung)
Tr	1 tablespoon dry sherry
0	1 teaspoon sesame oil
6	60 g (2 oz) snow peas (mange-tout)
7.5	**total grams carbohydrate**

Cut steak into paper-thin slices, across the grain of the beef. Combine the ginger, bean sauce, sherry and sesame oil and marinate the beef in the mixture for at least 1 hour. This may be done beforehand and the meat refrigerated.

Put meat into a heatproof dish, cover and steam over boiling water for 30–40 minutes, until beef is almost tender. Add snow peas to the dish and steam for a further few minutes. Serve with a vegetable dish or a small portion of rice.

Beef with Broccoli

Serves: 2

0	250 g (8 oz) beef fillet or rump (tenderloin or sirloin)
Tr	1 clove garlic, crushed
0	½ teaspoon salt
Tr	½ teaspoon grated fresh ginger
0	½ teaspoon five spice powder
10	250 g (8 oz) broccoli
2.5	1 teaspoon cornflour (cornstarch)
0	4 tablespoons water
2	1 tablespoon soy sauce
0	3 tablespoons peanut oil
0	2 teaspoons sesame oil
15.5	total grams carbohydrate

Cut beef into very thin slices, then cut slices into fine shreds. Remove any fat. Crush the garlic with the salt and rub garlic and grated ginger into beef, mixing thoroughly. Sprinkle the five spice powder over beef. Toss to distribute evenly. Slice broccoli thinly, or divide into small sprigs. Mix together the cornflour, water and soy sauce in a small bowl.

Heat oils in a wok and when hot add the beef and fry over high heat, stirring constantly, for 2 minutes or until meat changes colour. Add broccoli and fry for 3 minutes, stirring and tossing ingredients together all the time. Add cornflour mixture and stir until it boils and thickens, then stir well to coat beef and broccoli with sauce. Serve immediately.

Fried Beef and Long Beans

Serves: 3–4

6	12–15 long beans
0	375 g (12 oz) Scotch fillet or rump steak
Tr	1 clove garlic, crushed
Tr	½ teaspoon finely grated fresh ginger
0	½ teaspoon salt
9	½ teaspoon five spice powder
5	2 teaspoons cornflour (cornstarch)
0	1 tablespoon cold water
4	2 tablespoons oyster sauce
2	1 tablespoon soy sauce
0	2 tablespoons peanut oil
1	½ cup stock
19	total grams carbohydrate

Wash and cut beans into 5-cm (2-in) lengths. Shred beef finely and mix well with the garlic, ginger, salt and five spice powder. Mix cornflour smoothly with water, stir in oyster sauce and soy sauce.

Heat oil in a wok or heavy frying pan, add beef and beans and stir-fry over high heat for 2 minutes. Add stock and allow to simmer until beans are just tender, then stir in cornflour and sauce mixture and stir constantly until it boils and thickens. Toss the beef and beans in the sauce and serve at once.

Shredded Beef with Bean Sprouts

Serves: 5–6

0	500 g (1 lb) beef fillet or rump
Tr	1 clove garlic, crushed
0	½ teaspoon salt
Tr	½ teaspoon finely grated fresh ginger
2	1 teaspoon hoi sin sauce
2	1 tablespoon soy sauce
9	1 medium onion
3	½ green capsicum (sweet pepper)
10	250 g (8 oz) fresh bean sprouts
5	1 canned bamboo shoot
5	2 teaspoons cornflour (cornstarch)
0	2 tablespoons cold water
0	4 tablespoons peanut oil
8	½ cup canned salted walnuts
45	**total grams carbohydrate**

Cut beef into very thin shreds. Crush garlic with salt, combine with ginger, hoi sin sauce and soy sauce. Cut onion in half, lengthways, then into very thin lengthways slices. Dice capsicum. Wash and drain bean sprouts. Cut bamboo shoot into thin slices, then into squares. Mix cornflour and cold water and set aside.

Heat 2 tablespoons oil in a wok and fry onion and green pepper quickly, stirring all the time, until onion is soft and slightly coloured, about 3–4 minutes. Remove from pan. Heat remaining 2 tablespoons oil and fry beef on high heat, stirring and tossing constantly, until all the beef has lost its red colour and is turning brown. Add bean sprouts and bamboo shoot and toss until heated through, about 2 minutes. Move beef mixture to side of pan, add cornflour mixture to pan and stir until it boils and thickens. Return onions and capsicum to pan. Turn off heat, add walnuts and mix all together well.

Fillet of Beef in Black Bean Sauce

Serves: 2

0	250 g (8 oz) fillet or Scotch fillet (tenderloin)
1	1 tablespoon canned salted black beans
1	2 teaspoons soy sauce
0	4 tablespoons water
4	1 teaspoon sugar
5	125 g (4 oz) broccoli, sliced
0	1 tablespoon peanut oil
Tr	1 teaspoon crushed garlic
2.5	1 teaspoon cornflour (cornstarch)
0	1 tablespoon cold water
14	**total grams carbohydrate**

Substitute another suitable vegetable when broccoli is out of season, or prepare this dish without vegetables.

Cut beef in very thin slices and then into shreds, discarding any fat. Put black beans into a small strainer and rinse under running cold water for a few seconds. Drain, then mash with a fork. Combine beans with soy sauce, water and sugar. Peel broccoli stems and slice very finely. Divide flower heads into small sprigs. Bring lightly salted water to the boil in a small saucepan, drop in broccoli and return to boil. Boil for just 1 minute. Drain and rinse with cold water. Set aside.

Heat oil in a large wok and over high heat fry the beef, tossing and stirring constantly until colour changes. Add garlic, and toss for a few seconds, then add bean mixture. Bring to boil, then lower heat, cover and simmer for 2 minutes. Add cornflour mixed with cold water and stir until thickened, then add broccoli and stir until heated through, about 1 minute. Serve immediately with rice.

Stir-Fried Beef with Asparagus

Serves: 2–4

0	375 g (12 oz) lean steak
1	2 teaspoons light soy sauce
Tr	1 clove garlic, crushed
0	½ teaspoon salt
12	18 spears fresh tender asparagus
18	2 medium onions
0	4 tablespoons peanut oil
2	2 teaspoons Chinese bean sauce
	(see Glossary, page 181)
0	¼ cup water or stock
2.5	1 teaspoon cornflour (cornstarch)
0	1 tablespoon cold water
36	**total grams carbohydrate**

Trim all fat from steak and discard. Cut steak across the grain into paper-thin slices, then cut into bite-sized pieces. Sprinkle with soy sauce, mix in garlic crushed with salt. Leave aside.

Wash asparagus well in several changes of cold water, making sure any fine sand has been removed from the tips. Snap off tough ends of stalks. With a sharp knife cut into thin slices on the sharp diagonal so the slices are quite long and oval shaped. Keep the tips whole and set aside. Peel onions, cut in half lengthways, then cut each half into 4 or 6 wedges. Separate layers of onion.

Heat 2 tablespoons oil in a wok. Fry meat over high heat until colour changes. Remove it to a bowl. Wipe out wok, heat remaining 2 tablespoons oil and on high heat stir-fry the sliced asparagus stalks for 3 minutes. Add onion and fry for 1 minute longer. Add bean sauce and water or stock, and stir. Add the asparagus tips. Reduce heat, cover and cook for 3 minutes or until asparagus is just tender.

Push vegetables to side of pan. To the pan liquid add cornflour mixed smoothly with cold water. Stir and cook for 1 minute or until liquid boils and thickens. Return beef to pan, stir gently and heat through. Serve immediately with rice.

Pork with Salted Yellow Beans

0	1 pork chop, about 250 g (8 oz)
2	2 tablespoons salted yellow beans
1	1 teaspoon crushed garlic
1	1 teaspoon finely grated ginger
2	½ teaspoon sugar
0	2 tablespoons peanut oil
1	½ cup hot stock or water
2.5	1 teaspoon cornflour (cornstarch)
0	1 tablespoon cold water
9.5	**total grams carbohydrate**

Although labelled 'salted yellow beans' you will find, when you open the can, that they are a rich, dark brown.

Remove skin and excess fat and slice the pork chop into paper thin slices. Rinse the beans under cold water (hold them under the tap in a fine strainer) to remove excess saltiness. Put them on the chopping board and mash with Chinese chopper or fork. Mix the crushed garlic, grated ginger and sugar with the beans.

Heat wok, add 1 tablespoon oil and swirl to coat wok. Add the pork and fry on high heat, stirring constantly, until the pork loses every bit of pinkness. Move pork to side of wok, add remaining tablespoon oil and fry the bean mixture over medium heat, stirring, for 2–3 minutes. Add the stock, stir in the pork, cover and simmer for 3 minutes. Stir in the cornflour mixed smoothly with cold water and allow it to boil and thicken. Serve immediately with ½ cup portions of rice.

Stir-Fried Chilli Beef with Oyster Sauce

Serves: 2–4

0	250 g (8 oz) lean steak
0	1 tablespoon peanut oil
Tr	½ teaspoon finely chopped garlic
Tr	½ teaspoon finely chopped fresh ginger
6	½ cup thinly sliced spring onions (scallions)
Tr	1 teaspoon soy chilli sauce
6	12 snow peas (mange-tout) or ½ cup thinly sliced celery
1	½ teaspoon cornflour (cornstarch)
0	¼ cup water
0	1 teaspoon sesame oil
14.5	**total grams carbohydrate**

Cut the beef into paper-thin slices. Heat wok, add peanut oil and swirl to coat. Add garlic, ginger and half the spring onions. Stir-fry for 1 minute, add meat and stir-fry another minute on high heat. Add chilli sauce, snow peas (or celery) and stir-fry ½ minute. Mix cornflour with water and add to wok. Bring to boil, stirring, and add sesame oil. Add remaining spring onions. Mix thoroughly and serve with ½ cup portions of rice.

Note: If celery is used, the total grams of carbohydrate will be 10.5.

Stir-Fried Beef with Bean Sprouts

Serves: 2–4

0	250 g (8 oz) beef fillet or rump (tenderloin or sirloin)
Tr	1 clove garlic, crushed
0	1 teaspoon salt
Tr	½ teaspoon grated fresh ginger
0	½ teaspoon five spice powder
10	250 g (8 oz) bean sprouts
2.5	1 teaspoon cornflour (cornstarch)
0	2 tablespoons water
2	1 tablespoon soy sauce
0	1 tablespoon peanut oil
0	2 teaspoons sesame oil
15.5	**total grams carbohydrate**

Cut beef into very thin slices, then cut slices into fine shreds. Remove any fat. Crush the garlic with the salt and rub garlic, ginger and five spice powder into beef, mixing thoroughly. Wash bean sprouts and drain well. Mix together the cornflour, water and soy sauce.

Heat oils in a wok and when hot add the beef and fry over high heat, stirring constantly, for 2 minutes or until meat changes colour. Add bean sprouts and fry for 1 minute, stirring and tossing ingredients together all the time. Add cornflour mixture and stir until it boils and thickens slightly, then stir well to coat beef and bean sprouts with sauce. Serve immediately.

Stir-Fried Beef with Cucumber

Serves: 2

0	250 g (8 oz) lean steak
Tr	1 clove garlic, crushed
0	½ teaspoon salt
Tr	½ teaspoon finely grated fresh ginger
8	1 large green cucumber
0	1 tablespoon peanut oil
2	3 spring onions (scallions), cut into 2.5-cm (1-in) pieces
11	**total grams carbohydrate**

Cut beef into paper-thin slices. Combine garlic, salt and ginger and rub into the beef. Peel cucumber thinly, leaving a trace of green. Cut in halves lengthways, scoop out and discard seeds and cut each half into diagonal slices.

Heat peanut oil in wok and fry the beef on high heat until it changes colour. Add the cucumber and stir-fry for 1 minute, then add spring onions and toss together for a minute longer. Serve hot.

Stir-Fried Beef with Capsicums (Sweet Peppers) *Serves: 2–4*

0	250 g (8 oz) beef fillet or rump (tenderloin or siloin)
Tr	I clove garlic, crushed
0	½ teaspoon salt
Tr	½ teaspoon grated fresh ginger
0	½ teaspoon five spice powder
4	I red capsicum (sweet pepper)
4	I green capsicum (sweet pepper)
2.5	I teaspoon cornflour (cornstarch)
0	2 tablespoons water
2	I tablespoon soy sauce
0	I tablespoon peanut oil
0	2 teaspoons sesame oil

13.5	total grams carbohydrate

Cut beef into very thin slices, then cut slices into fine shreds. Remove any fat. Crush the garlic with ½ teaspoon salt and rub garlic and ginger into beef, mixing thoroughly. Sprinkle five spice powder over beef and toss to distribute evenly. Cut capsicums into fine slices. Mix together the cornflour, water and soy sauce.

Heat oils in a wok and when hot add the beef and fry over high heat, stirring constantly, for 2 minutes or until meat changes colour. Add capsicum slices and fry for 1 minute, sprinkle with remaining salt and toss ingredients together. Add cornflour mixture and stir until it boils and thickens slightly, then stir to coat beef and capsicum. Serve immediately.

Stir-Fried Beef with Capsicums (Sweet Peppers)

Meatballs with Water Chestnuts and Celery

Meatballs with Water Chestnuts and Celery

Serves: 4–6

0	500 g (1 lb) ground lean beef or pork and veal mince
Tr	½ teaspoon crushed garlic
1	1 teaspoon finely grated fresh ginger
0	½ teaspoon salt
0	½ teaspoon pepper
2	1 tablespoon light soy sauce
5	2 teaspoons cornflour (cornstarch)
Tr	1 small egg, beaten
7	2 tablespoons finely chopped water chestnuts
0	2 tablespoons peanut oil
2	1 tablespoon dark soy sauce
Tr	1 tablespoon dry sherry
0	½ teaspoon sesame oil
0	¼ cup water
4	1 cup finely sliced celery
12	5 water chestnuts, sliced into rounds
6	3 spring onions (scallions), cut into bite-sized lengths
5.2	½ cup sliced bamboo shoot, optional
45.7	**total grams carbohydrate**

Combine minced meat with garlic, ginger, salt, pepper and soy sauce mixed with cornflour. Add egg and chopped water chestnuts and mix thoroughly. With lightly oiled hands, form into 24–30 small balls.

Heat peanut oil in a wok or frying pan and brown the meatballs. Lower heat, cover and simmer until done. Thread two meatballs on each skewer, using short bamboo skewers. Heat the dark soy sauce, sherry, sesame oil and water. Add celery, water chestnuts, spring onions and bamboo shoot and cook on high heat, stirring, for 1 minute. Spoon over meatballs and serve hot.

Mongolian Lamb

Mongolian Lamb

Serves: 4

0	500 g (1 lb) trimmed lamb, loin, topside or round
8	2 teaspoons sugar
0	1 teaspoon salt
4	2 tablespoons dark soy sauce
Tr	1 small egg
0	¼ teaspoon bicarbonate of soda
5	2 teaspoons cornflour (cornstarch)
0	3 tablespoons peanut oil
1	1 teaspoon finely chopped garlic
2	1 spring onion (scallion), finely sliced
0	¼ teaspoon five spice powder
4	2 teaspoons hoi sin sauce
1	1 teaspoon chilli bean sauce
Tr	1 tablespoon dry sherry

26	total grams carbohydrate

Trim away all fat, skin and gristle and cut the lean meat into bite-sized, paper-thin slices. Soak in cold water for 30 minutes. Rinse until water runs clear, then drain well and squeeze out excess water. Add sugar, salt, soy sauce, egg, bicarbonate of soda (for tenderising) and cornflour. Mix well, then add 1 tablespoon of the peanut oil and mix again. Leave to marinate at least 2 hours.

Heat a wok, add 1 tablespoon peanut oil, and on very high heat stir-fry the lamb until colour changes. Remove lamb from wok. Heat remaining 1 tablespoon oil over low heat, add garlic and spring onion and cook gently until they start to colour. Add the five spice powder, hoi sin sauce and chilli bean sauce, return lamb to wok, and toss over high heat. Add sherry, mix, then serve at once.

Stir-Fried Beef with Onion and Mushrooms

Serves: 4

2	6 dried Chinese mushrooms
0	375 g (12 oz) lean beef steak, thinly sliced
0	¼ teaspoon five spice powder
0	½ teaspoon salt
Tr	1 clove garlic, crushed
Tr	½ teaspoon finely grated ginger
0	3 tablespoons peanut oil
9	1 onion, cut in eighths
4	2 tablespoons dark soy sauce
0	¼ cup water or stock
2.5	1 teaspoon cornflour (cornstarch)
0	1 tablespoon cold water
0	spring onions (scallions) for garnish
18.5	**total grams carbohydrate**

Soak mushrooms in hot water for 20–30 minutes. Cut off and discard stems, slice caps thinly. Slice beef paper-thin in bite-sized lengths. Sprinkle with five spice powder and salt, add garlic and ginger and mix well.

Heat 1 tablespoon oil in wok, fry onions and mushrooms for 2–3 minutes, remove from wok. Add remaining 2 tablespoons oil and when hot add beef and fry on high heat, stirring and tossing, until beef changes colour. Add soy sauce and stock, bring to the boil, then thicken slightly with cornflour blended with cold water. Turn off heat and stir in the onions and mushrooms. Serve garnished with spring onions.

Braised Pork with Cabbage

Serves: 4–5

2	6 dried mushrooms
Tr	1 tablespoon dried wood fungus
0	500 g (1 lb) pork shoulder
3	1½ tablespoons soy sauce
Tr	1 tablespoon brandy or Chinese wine
5	2 teaspoons cornflour (cornstarch)
0	2 tablespoons peanut oil
1	2 cloves garlic, crushed
0	2 cups hot water
4	2 tablespoons oyster sauce
6	250 g (8 oz) mustard cabbage or white cabbage
21.5	**total grams carbohydrate**

Soak mushrooms in hot water for 30 minutes. Soak wood fungus in cold water. Cut pork into thin slices. Combine soy sauce, wine and cornflour and mix well with pork.

Heat peanut oil in a wok, add garlic, then turn in pork and fry for a few minutes, stirring. Add mushrooms, sliced, and the hot water and oyster sauce. Cover and simmer 35 minutes or until pork is tender.

Meanwhile slice cabbage into bite-sized pieces. When pork is cooked, add cabbage and wood fungus and cook for 2 minutes longer. Serve with ½ cup portions of rice or noodles.

Barbecue-style Pork with Black Beans

Serves: 4–5

0	500 g (1 lb) boneless loin of pork
1	2 cloves garlic
0	¼ teaspoon salt
1	1 teaspoon finely grated fresh ginger
12	2 teaspoons honey
Tr	1 tablespoon Chinese wine or dry sherry
0	½ teaspoon five spice powder
1	1 tablespoon black beans, chopped
2	1 tablespoon dark soy sauce
0	1 tablespoon peanut oil

17.5   total grams carbohydrate

Ask the butcher to remove rind from the pork. Cut pork into strips 5 cm (2 in) long and 2.5 cm (1 in) wide. Crush garlic with salt and combine with all the other ingredients except oil. Rub over the pork and leave for at least 15 minutes to marinate.

Heat wok, add oil and swirl to coat wok. Add the pork pieces, reserving marinade. Stir-fry the pork until browned, then add reserved marinade. Swirl ½ cup hot water in the bowl and add that too. Reduce heat, cover and simmer for 30–40 minutes until pork is tender. Stir occasionally and add more hot water if liquid looks like drying up. Be careful that the sweet marinade does not burn. The heat should be very low throughout the cooking.

When pork is tender remove from heat and if not serving straight away it may be reheated at serving time. Serve with plain white rice.

Note: A larger quantity of pork can be cooked like this, and part of it refrigerated and used for adding to dishes that call for a small amount of barbecued pork.

Pork with Abalone, Sichuan-Style

Serves: 4–6

0	250 g (8 oz) lean pork fillet
5	1 x 454 g (16 oz) can abalone
0	2 tablespoons peanut oil
1	1 teaspoon finely chopped fresh ginger
Tr	1 clove garlic, finely chopped
2.5	1 teaspoon cornflour (cornstarch)
0	1 tablespoon cold water
1	1 teaspoon chilli sauce
10	**total grams carbohydrate**

Cut pork fillet into very thin slices. Drain canned abalone, reserving liquid from can. Cut abalone into paper thin slices.

Heat oil in wok with ginger and garlic, add pork and stir-fry over high heat until colour changes. Add ½ cup liquid from can of abalone, cover and simmer for 10 minutes. Add cornflour mixed with cold water, stir until boiling and thickened, then stir in chilli sauce. Mix well. Add abalone slices and leave only just long enough to heat through, about 1 minute. Abalone must not be over-cooked or it will be tough. Serve with ½ cup portions of boiled rice or noodles.

Barbecued Pork

Serves: 4–6

See picture on page 24

0	500 g (1 lb) pork fillet or belly
1	3 cloves garlic
0	1 teaspoon salt
Tr	½ teaspoon finely grated ginger
2	1 tablespoon soy sauce
24	1 tablespoon honey
Tr	1 tablespoon Chinese wine or sherry
0	½ teaspoon five spice powder
28	**total grams carbohydrate**

With a sharp knife remove rind from pork, or ask butcher to do this for you. Cut pork into strips the length of the piece of pork and about 2.5 cm (1 in) wide. Crush garlic with salt and combine with all the other ingredients in a large bowl. Put in the pork, mix well together so that pork is covered on all sides with the marinade. Allow to marinate for 15 minutes or longer.

Preheat oven to 200–230°C (400–450°F). Half fill a roasting pan with hot water and place a wire rack across the top. Place pork on rack and roast in hot oven for 30 minutes. Turn pork strips over, brush with remaining marinade and cook further 15 minutes or until well glazed and lightly touched with dark brown on the spots where the honey marinade has caramelised. Cut into bite-sized slices to serve. Serve warm or at room temperature.

Stir-Fried Veal and Vegetables

Serves: 4

0	375 g (12 oz) veal cutlets
Tr	1 teaspoon crushed garlic
Tr	1 teaspoon finely grated fresh ginger
4	2 tablespoons light soy sauce
Tr	2 teaspoons sherry, optional
1	1 large stalk celery
3	1 small green capsicum (sweet pepper)
3	1 small red capsicum (sweet pepper)
2	1 small winter bamboo shoot, optional
8	4 spring onions (scallions)
12	1 small, firm lettuce
0	2 tablespoons peanut oil
0	salt to taste

34.5   total grams carbohydrate

Veal is not used in traditional Chinese cooking, but this recipe came about because of what was in the refrigerator and it was too easy and delicious not to include. Pork schnitzel or yearling steak may be used instead of veal.

Slice the veal into thin strips. Mix half the garlic and ginger with 1 tablespoon of the soy sauce and the sherry, if used. Pour it over the veal and set aside. String celery and cut into thin strips. Remove stalks and seeds from capsicums and cut into thin strips. Cut bamboo shoot into thin strips, and spring onions into bite-sized lengths. Have these vegetables ready on a plate. Cut the lettuce in halves lengthways, then cut each half into three strips and across into three again so there are nine chunky pieces in each half. Keep lettuce separate from other vegetables.

Heat 1 tablespoon oil in a wok and when very hot swirl to coat inner surface of wok with oil. Add the remaining garlic and ginger and the mixed vegetables and stir-fry over high heat for 1 minute or until all the vegetables have come in contact with the oil and the heat. At the most this step should take 2 minutes. Add the lettuce, stir-fry for a further 30 seconds, then sprinkle with remaining tablespoon of soy sauce, turn heat down to low, cover and allow to steam for 1 minute. Remove all the vegetables to a dish. Wipe out pan with paper, heat remaining tablespoon oil and when very hot add the marinated veal and stir-fry on high heat until meat changes colour. Turn heat to medium, allow to simmer for 1 minute, then return vegetables and toss together. Taste, and add salt if necessary. Serve at once.

Pork with Lotus Root

Serves: 2–4

0	250 g (8 oz) pork fillet
2	1 tablespoon light soy sauce
0	½ teaspoon salt
Tr	½ teaspoon crushed garlic
Tr	½ teaspoon finely grated fresh ginger
2	1 teaspoon hoi sin sauce
0	2 tablespoons peanut oil
0	⅓ cup stock or water
2.5	1 teaspoon cornflour (cornstarch)
0	2 teaspoons cold water
3	5 slices frozen or canned lotus root
4	12 green beans, cut into bite-sized pieces
0	spring onion (scallion) flowers or fresh coriander (cilantro) sprigs for garnish
14.5	**total grams carbohydrate**

Partially freeze pork and cut into paper-thin slices. Combine soy sauce, salt, garlic, ginger and hoi sin sauce and mix with the pork.

Heat oil in a wok and swirl to coat wok. When very hot add the pork and stir-fry over high heat until all the pieces have come in contact with the hot wok and the colour is no longer pink. Add stock and bring to the boil, cover and simmer 2 minutes. Stir in cornflour mixed with water until it boils and thickens slightly. Add lotus root and heat in the sauce. Arrange on a plate and garnish with spring onion flowers or sprigs of fresh coriander. Serve hot with ½ cup portions of rice.

Pork with Lotus Root

Minced Veal in Lettuce Rolls

Serves: 4–6

0	500 g (1 lb) minced (ground veal
0	1 tablespoon peanut oil
1	1 teaspoon finely chopped garlic
1	1 teaspoon finely chopped fresh ginger
2.6	¼ cup finely chopped bamboo shoot
10.5	¼ cup chopped water chestnuts
2	6 dried Chinese mushrooms, soaked and chopped
2	1 tablespoon dark soy sauce
0	¼ teaspoon five spice powder
0	¼ teaspoon ground black pepper
2.5	1 teaspoon cornflour (cornstarch)
0	2 teaspoons cold water
4	2 spring onions (scallions), finely sliced
3.6	12 crisp lettuce leaves
29.2	total grams carbohydrate

Heat peanut oil and fry garlic and ginger over low heat until just golden, then add veal and fry on high heat, stirring constantly, until veal loses its pinkness. Add the bamboo shoot, water chestnuts, mushrooms and mix well. Add soy sauce, five spice powder and pepper, mix well, then turn heat low, add stock, cover and cook until very little liquid remains.

Make a well in the middle, add cornflour mixed with water and stir until it boils and thickens slightly. Mix through beal. Serve garnished with spring onions and accompanied by lettuce leaves. A portion of mince is wrapped in a leaf, which is rolled to enclose the meat and eaten like a spring roll.

Note: This recipe is very similar to Lettuce Rolls with Pork and Prawns (see recipe and picture on page 20-21).

Spiced Spareribs

0	1.5 kg (3 lb) pork spareribs
2	4 cloves garlic
0	1½ teaspoons salt
0	½ teaspoon ground black pepper
0	½ teaspoon five spice powder
12	2 teaspoons honey
0	1 tablespoon sesame oil
6	3 tablespoons light soy sauce
0	½ cup hot water
	plum sauce for serving, optional
	(8 grams carbohydrate per tablespoon)
20	**total grams carbohydrate**

Prepare this when you have guests—it's hardly worth making a smaller quantity. But pork is a rich meat and needs to be eaten with rice, so weight-conscious people should keep the servings small and go very easy on the plum sauce—it has loads of sugar in it. It can be prepared a day ahead. When required, grill the spareribs a few minutes on each side, just to heat through. The best way to enjoy spareribs is to pick them up in the fingers.

Preheat oven to 180–190°C (350–375°F). Separate spare ribs with a sharp knife or ask the butcher to do it for you. Crush garlic with salt, combine with pepper, five spice powder, honey, sesame oil and soy sauce. Rub well into spareribs. Put them in a roasting pan and cook in a moderate oven. After 30 minutes, turn spareribs, add hot water to pan and continue roasting, basting with the liquid every 10 minutes, for a further 30 minutes.

Alternatively, heat 1–2 tablespoons peanut oil in a large heavy frying pan and brown spareribs. Add water, cover and simmer for 30–35 minutes or until tender.

Serve hot with plum sauce and boiled rice.

Vegetables

This is a chapter that will guide you through a lot of traps for the unwary. Although vegetables are low in calories, some are surprisingly high in carbohydrates. Avoid root vegetables which are mainly starchy. Water chestnuts, with their delicious crunch, are an ingredient I couldn't bear to drop altogether, but they do have to be used with discretion because they have a fairly high carbohydrate count. The same applies to bamboo shoot. Measure as stated in each recipe. Even snow peas, with their delicate sweetness, are to be added in moderation.

Celery, capsicums, cauliflower and mushrooms are among the safest vegetables to eat on this diet.

Kidneys with Bamboo Shoots and Walnuts

Serves: 4–6

4	500 g (1 lb) pork, lamb or veal kidneys
0	1 teaspoon salt
0	4 tablespoons peanut oil
4	¼ cup peeled walnuts
Tr	1 clove garlic, finely chopped
2	2 teaspoons soy chili sauce
2	1 tablespoon dark soy sauce
Tr	1 tablespoon dry sherry
10.4	1 cup finely sliced bamboo shoot
8	4 spring onions (scallions), cut into bite-sized lengths
31.4	**total grams carbohydrate**

Wash the kidneys, remove cores and cut the kidneys into paper-thin slices. If large, cut to bite-sized. Wash the kidneys under running cold water, then put into a large bowl, cover with cold water, add salt and leave to soak for half an hour. Drain, wash well until there is no trace of blood in the water. Drain and blot on paper towels. Bring about 5 cups lightly salted water to the boil, drop in the kidney slices and bring back to the boil. Boil for 1 minute, drain in a colander and then spread on kitchen paper and blot dry again.

Heat peanut oil in a wok and fry the walnuts on low heat just until they turn golden. Drain on absorbent paper. Pour off half the oil, leaving only 2 tablespoons in wok. Fry the garlic, stirring, until golden, then add the sauces, sherry, bamboo shoot, spring onions and kidneys. Stir-fry for 2 minutes, mix in the walnuts and serve hot with small portions of rice.

Kidneys in Black Bean Sauce

Serves: 4–6

4	500 g (1 lb) pork, lamb or veal kidneys
4	1 red capsicum (sweet pepper)
2	2 tablespoons canned salted black beans
1	2 cloves garlic
4	1 teaspoon sugar
0	2 tablespoons peanut oil
1	1 teaspoon finely grated fresh ginger
0	¼ cup water
16	**total grams carbohydrate**

Wash the kidneys, remove core and cut them into paper-thin slices. If the slices are large, cut to bite-sized. Wash the kidneys under running cold water, then put into a large bowl, cover with cold water and leave to soak for half an hour. Drain, wash well once more until there is no trace of blood in the water. Drop into a saucepan of lightly salted boiling water, boil for 1 minute. Drain well and blot on paper towels.

Discard seeds and membrane and cut capsicum into thin slices. Mash beans with fork. Crush garlic with sugar and mix with the mashed beans. Heat peanut oil and stir-fry the ginger and capsicum for a few seconds, then add the bean mixture and fry for a few seconds longer. Add the water and stir while bringing to the boil, then add kidneys and cook, stirring, until they are coated with the bean sauce. Serve at once with small portions of rice.

Bamboo Shoots, Snow Peas and Cucumber

Serves: 2–4

10.4	1 cup sliced winter bamboo shoots
12	125 g (4 oz) snow peas
6	1 cucumber
0	1 tablespoon peanut oil
0	1 teaspoon sesame oil
Tr	¼ teaspoon crushed garlic
Tr	¼ teaspoon finely grated fresh ginger
Tr	1 teaspoon light soy sauce
0	salt to taste
29.9	**total grams carbohydrate**

Slice the bamboo shoots thinly. Remove stems and strings from snow peas. Peel and cut cucumber into thin slices.

Heat peanut oil in a wok, add sesame oil, garlic and ginger and stir once, then turn in bamboo shoots and snow peas. Stir-fry for 1 minute over high heat. Add cucumber slices and cook 2 minutes longer. Add soy sauce and salt. Serve at once.

Note: Winter bamboo shoots, or green bamboo shoots, are smaller, whiter and more tender than the usual variety. If not available substitute the larger kind.

Heavenly Braised Vegetables

Serves: 4–6

6	12 dried Chinese mushrooms
1	3 tablespoons dried wood fungus (wan yee)
14	1 x 238 g (8½ oz) can bamboo shoot
29	1 x 425 g (15 oz) can young corn cobs
0	2 tablespoons peanut oil
4	2 tablespoons soy sauce
4	1 teaspoon sugar
0	2 cups mushroom liquid
0	1 tablespoon sesame oil
58	**total grams carbohydrate**

Soak mushrooms in 3 cups hot water for 30 minutes. Squeeze out excess moisture, remove and discard stems. Reserve mushroom liquid. Soak fungus in water for 10 minutes, rinse and drain, then cut each piece in two. Slice bamboo shoots thinly. Drain corn.

Heat peanut oil in a wok and fry mushrooms until brown, about 5 minutes on high heat, stirring all the time. Add remaining ingredients, except wood fungus. Add mushroom liquid, cover and simmer over low heat for 25–30 minutes. Add wood fungus and heat briefly. Sprinkle sesame oil over and toss to mix flavour through.

Broccoli, Bean Sprouts and Water Chestnuts

Serves: 6

24	500 g (1 lb) fresh broccoli
10	250 g (8 oz) fresh bean sprouts
19	8 water chestnuts, fresh or canned

DRESSING

0	1 tablespoon sesame oil
0	2 tablespoons peanut oil
6	3 tablespoons light soy sauce
2	½ teaspoon sugar, optional

63	total grams carbohydrate

Separate broccoli into small sprigs, trimming off all but the most tender stems. Bring a small pan of lightly salted water to the boil, drop in broccoli, return to the boil and boil for 1 minute. Drain, then rinse under running cold water to stop cooking and set the colour. Wash bean sprouts in cold water and drain in colander. Slice the canned water chestnuts, or peel and slice fresh ones. Toss well together with combined dressing ingredients.

Braised Cauliflower

Serves: 2–4

12	2 cups cauliflower sprigs
0	2 tablespoons peanut oil
Tr	½ teaspoon finely grated fresh ginger
2	1 tablespoon light soy sauce
0	¼ cup water
0	1 teaspoon sesame oil
2	1 spring onion (scallion), finely sliced

16.5	total grams carbohydrate

Cauliflower is a good vegetable to use while dieting because it is low in carbohydrates, has a crisp texture when short-cooked and does a remarkable job of filling you up without resorting to starches.

Use only the tender florets of the cauliflower; wash and drain well.

Heat wok, add peanut oil and swirl around, then add ginger and cauliflower and toss over high heat for 30 seconds. Add soy sauce and water mixed together, cover and cook on high heat for 3 minutes. (Test cauliflower—it should be tender but still slightly firm and crisp.) Stir until liquid has almost evaporated, remove from heat, sprinkle sesame oil over, add spring onion and toss. Serve hot.

Broccoli, Bean Sprouts and Water Chestnuts

Braised Vegetable Combination

12	125 g (4 oz) dried bean curd or gluten steak or dried soy bean protein
6	12 dried Chinese mushrooms
3	30 dried lily buds (golden needles)
Tr	2 tablespoons dried wood fungus
6.2	125 g (4 oz) canned bamboo shoot
14	125 g (4 oz) canned lotus root
0	3 tablespoons peanut oil
4	2 tablespoons light soy sauce
4	2 teaspoons hoi sin sauce
0	1½ cups mushroom soaking liquid
0	3 sections star anise
0	2 teaspoons sesame oil
8	2 teaspoons sugar
5	2 teaspoons cornflour (cornstarch)
0	2 tablespoons cold water

62.7	total grams carbohydrate

This is a favourite dish for vegetarians.

Break bean curd into bite-sized pieces and soak in cold water for 20 minutes. Drain, pour boiling water over and allow to stand for a further 20 minutes. Drain well. Wash mushrooms and soak in hot water for 30 minutes. Drain, reserve the liquid, remove stems, squeeze out excess moisture from caps. If large, cut caps in halves. Soak lily buds in hot water for 30 minutes, drain, pinch off tough stem ends if necessary and either tie a knot in each one or cut in halves.

Soak wood fungus in hot water for 10 minutes, drain and cut into bite-sized pieces. Cut bamboo shoot and lotus root into thin slices, then into bite-sized pieces.

Heat a wok, pour in peanut oil and swirl to coat wok. When very hot add bean curd, mushrooms and lily buds and stir-fry for 3–4 minutes over medium high heat. Add the soy and hoi sin sauces, stirred into 1½ cups mushroom liquid. Add star anise. Bring to the boil, turn heat low, cover and simmer 15 minutes. Add bamboo shoot, lotus root, sesame oil and sugar, stir well, cover and simmer 10 minutes longer. If liquid evaporates too rapidly add more mushroom liquid or hot water. Remove star anise.

Mix cornflour smoothly with cold water and stir into liquid. Cook until it becomes clear and thickens slightly. Add wood fungus and push other vegetables to side of pan, allowing fungus to heat through. Serve hot with rice.

Note: Prepare gluten steaks or dried soy bean protein according to instructions on label. For a non-vegetarian version, the bean curd or substitute may be replaced with 250 g (8 oz) beef or pork cut into small cubes.

Bean Curd with Crab Sauce

Serves: 2

1	125 g (4 oz) crab meat, fresh, frozen or canned
0	1 tablespoon peanut oil
8	4 spring onions (scallions), roughly chopped
Tr	½ teaspoon finely grated fresh ginger
Tr	¼ cup chicken or fish stock (page 150)
0	small pinch of pepper
2.5	1 teaspoon cornflour (cornstarch)
0	1 tablespoon cold water
3.6	4 squares fresh bean curd
16.1	total grams carbohydrate

Drain and flake crab and pick over to remove any bony tissue. Heat the oil in a small pan and gently fry spring onions and ginger for a minute or so, stirring, until ginger starts to turn golden and spring onions are softened. Add stock, cover and simmer for 3–4 minutes. Add crab meat and heat through. Season with pepper, then stir in cornflour mixed to a smooth paste with cold water. Stir over medium heat until sauce boils and thickens. Add bean curd, spoon sauce over and heat until just about to come to the boil. Do not over-cook. Taste and add salt if necessary. Serve at once with rice.

Stir-Fried Spinach

Serves: 2–4

13.5	1 bunch spinach
0	2 tablespoons peanut oil
Tr	1 teaspoon crushed garlic
2	1 tablespoon light soy sauce
2	½ teaspoon sugar
0	1 teaspoon sesame oil
18	total grams carbohydrate

Wash spinach in several changes of water. With a sharp knife remove tough stems. Roll the leaves into a firm bunch and shred finely with a stainless steel knife. Heat peanut oil in a wok and on medium heat fry the garlic for a few seconds. Add the spinach and toss over medium heat for 30 seconds, then sprinkle with a mixture of the soy sauce, sugar and sesame oil and toss again to distribute the seasonings. Cooking time should be very short so that the leaves are still bright green. Serve at once.

Braised Mushrooms

8	60 g (2 oz) dried Chinese mushrooms (about 24 medium-sized mushrooms)
0	2 cups hot water
4	2 tablespoons dark soy sauce
12	3 teaspoons sugar
0	1 tablespoon sesame oil
0	3 tablespoons peanut oil
24	total grams carbohydrate

To be served as part of the cold hors d'oeuvre platter (see page 24)

Wash mushrooms well in cold water. Put in a bowl, pour hot water over and soak for 20 minutes. With a sharp knife, cut off stems and discard. Squeeze as much water as possible from mushrooms, reserving the liquid. To the reserved liquid, add enough of the water in which the mushrooms were soaked to make 1½ cups. Add soy sauce, sugar, sesame oil and stir to dissolve sugar.

Heat peanut oil in a small wok and fry mushrooms over a high heat, stirring and turning, until the undersides are browned. Add liquid mixture, reduce heat, cover and simmer for approximately 30 minutes or until all the liquid is absorbed and the mushrooms take on a shiny appearance. Towards end of cooking time it is advisable to stir occasionally. Serve hot or cold.

Note: Braised mushrooms, either whole or sliced, can also be added to other dishes.

Braised Mushrooms

Bean Curd Braised in Oyster Sauce

Serves: 2–3

0	1 tablespoon peanut oil
Tr	1 small clove garlic, crushed
5.6	250 g (8 oz) Chinese cabbage or mixed vegetables
Tr	2 tablespoons stock
2	1 tablespoon oyster sauce
2	1 tablespoon soy sauce
Tr	1 tablespoon sherry
2.5	1 teaspoon cornflour (cornstarch)
0	1 tablespoon water
3.6	4 squares fresh bean curd
17.2	total grams carbohydrate

Heat oil in a wok and gently fry the garlic for 1 minute. Add vegetables cut in bite-sized pieces and stir-fry on high heat for 2 minutes. Add stock, cover and simmer for 1 minute longer. Mix together the oyster sauce, soy sauce and sherry. Add to wok, stir and simmer. Add cornflour mixed with cold water, and stir until it boils and thickens. Add squares of bean curd, heat through and serve immediately with boiled rice.

Stir-Fried Green Vegetables

Serves: 2–4

8	1 cup sliced green beans
10	2 cups broccoli sprigs
8	1 cup brussels sprouts, quartered
0	1 tablespoon peanut oil
Tr	1 clove garlic, crushed
Tr	½ teaspoon finely grated fresh ginger
0	½ teaspoon salt
1	½ cup chicken stock (see page 156) or hot water
0	2 teaspoons sesame oil
28	total grams carbohydrate

String the beans and cut in thin diagonal slices. Slit stems of broccoli to allow heat to penetrate. Quarter sprouts lengthways, keeping a bit of centre stem on each piece.

Heat wok, add oil and swirl to coat, add garlic and ginger and stir for a few seconds. Add vegetables and toss over high heat, until the vegetables turn a brilliant green. Add salt and stock, cover and steam for 2 minutes. Vegetables should be half-cooked and still crisp and crunchy. Sprinkle sesame oil over, toss and serve at once or the vegetables will lose their texture and bright colour.

Bean Curd Braised in Oyster Sauce

Vegetarian Egg Foo Yong

Serves: 2–4

2	4 dried Chinese mushrooms
2	4 eggs
0	¼ teaspoon salt
0	⅛ teaspoon pepper
4	2 spring onions (scallions), finely chopped
14	6 water chestnuts, chopped
6	1 cup fresh bean sprouts
Tr	1 teaspoon light soy sauce
0	1 tablespoon peanut oil
28.5	total grams carbohydrate

Soak the mushrooms in hot water for 30 minutes, squeeze out excess water, discard stems. Chop mushroom caps finely. Beat the eggs until well mixed but not frothy, season with salt and pepper and stir in all the other ingredients, except oil.

Heat a wok, add a teaspoon of oil and swirl to coat a small area at base of wok. Add about ¼ cup egg mixture and cook on medium low heat until lightly browned on underside. Turn and cook until other side is set. Remove to a warm plate. Repeat with rest of mixture until all the omelettes are made. Serve hot, 2–3 to a serving.

Stir-Fried Vegetables with Sauce

Serves: 2–4

11.2	500 g (1 lb) Chinese cabbage of any kind
2	1 large white radish
0	2 tablespoons peanut oil
0	1 tablespoon sesame oil
Tr	1 teaspoon finely grated fresh ginger
Tr	1 teaspoon crushed garlic
4	2 tablespoons light soy sauce
Tr	2 teaspoons vinegar
4	1 teaspoon sugar
1.2	½ teaspoon cornflour (cornstarch)
0	2 teaspoons cold water
23.9	total grams carbohydrate

Use the large mild radish, called Daikon in Japanese and Loh bak in Chinese. Better still, try to get some of the miniature white turnips no larger than round red radishes.

Wash the cabbage thoroughly and cut the stems, including part of the green leaves, into diagonal slices. Cut radish into thin bite-sized slices.

Heat peanut oil in a wok and when very hot swirl to coat the wok then add the vegetables. Stir-fry on high heat for 1–2 minutes. Cabbage should still be crisp and green. Remove from wok.

Add the sesame oil and on medium heat fry the ginger and garlic, stirring, just until they start to colour. Add the soy sauce, vinegar and sugar and stir to dissolve sugar. Thicken slightly with cornflour mixed with 2 teaspoons cold water. Return vegetables to wok and toss to coat lightly with the seasonings. Serve hot.

Broccoli Stems with Oyster Sauce

Serves: 2–4

10	2 cups thick stems of broccoli
0	2 tablespoons peanut oil
Tr	I clove garlic, crushed
2	I tablespoon oyster sauce
12.5	total grams carbohydrate

Peel the broccoli stems and slice them into bite-sized pieces. Put 2 cups water into a wok and bring to a rolling boil, drop in the stems, cover and cook for I minute, no longer. Drain in a colander and run cold water over to stop cooking. Dry the wok over heat, add the peanut oil and fry the garlic for a few seconds, stirring, until it is pale golden. Add the oyster sauce and return the broccoli stems to the wok, stirring and tossing until they are thinly coated with the sauce. Serve at once.

Stir-Fried Bean Sprouts

Serves: 2–4

18	3 cups fresh bean sprouts
0	2 tablespoons peanut oil
Tr	½ teaspoon crushed garlic
Tr	½ teaspoon finely grated fresh ginger
0	½ teaspoon salt
0	2 teaspoons sesame oil
2	I spring onion (scallion), cut in fine diagonal slices
21	total grams carbohydrate

Wash bean sprouts in cold water, and pinch off any straggly brown tails. Drain thoroughly.

Heat a wok, pour in the oil and swirl to coat, then fry garlic and ginger on low heat for a few seconds, stirring, just until pale golden. Add the bean sprouts and stir-fry for I minute or less, just until the beans are tossed in the flavoured oil. Remove from heat. Sprinkle with salt and sesame oil, toss to distribute the seasoning and serve immediately, garnished with the sliced spring onion.

Quick-Fried Long Beans

Quick-Fried Long Beans

Serves: 4–6

39	500 g (1 lb) long beans
0	1 tablespoon peanut oil
Tr	1 small clove garlic, crushed
Tr	½ teaspoon finely grated fresh ginger
0	1 teaspoon sesame oil
0	½ teaspoon salt
40	total grams carbohydrate

Wash and cut beans into 5-cm (2-in) lengths. Heat oil in a wok or frying pan and add garlic, ginger and beans. Fry, stirring constantly over high heat, for 2 minutes or until just tender. Stir in sesame oil and salt. Serve at once.

Mixed Braised Vegetables

Serves: 2–4

0	2 tablespoons peanut oil
0	1 teaspoon sesame oil
Tr	1 large clove garlic, crushed
Tr	1 teaspoon grated fresh ginger
16	500 g (1 lb) sliced vegetables
0	½ cup hot water or light stock
2	1 tablespoon oyster sauce
1	2 teaspoons light soy sauce
0	½ teaspoon salt
2.5	1 teaspoon cornflour (cornstarch)
0	1 tablespoon cold water
22.5	total grams carbohydrate

Use a mixture of white Chinese cabbage, mustard cabbage, leeks, cauliflower, spring onions and beans in any combination or proportions. Weigh after trimming and slicing. The carbohydrate count will vary according to the type of vegetables used.

Heat oils in a wok with garlic and ginger, add vegetables and stir-fry for 2 minutes. Add hot water or stock and sauces and salt mixed together. Cover and simmer for 4 minutes. Push vegetables to side of wok, add cornflour mixed with cold water, stir until slightly thickened. Toss vegetables in sauce and serve immediately.

Stuffed Bitter Melon in Black Bean Sauce

Serves: 2–3

16	250 g (8 oz) bitter melon
0	500 g (1 lb) fillet of bream or other white fish
0	125 g (4 oz) raw prawns
0	¼ teaspoon salt
Tr	½ teaspoon finely grated fresh ginger
Tr	1 tablespoon egg white
2.5	1 teaspoon cornflour (cornstarch)
0	4 tablespoons peanut oil

SAUCE

2	2 tablespoons canned salted black beans
Tr	1 clove garlic, crushed
2.5	1 teaspoon sugar
0	½ cup light stock or water
4	1½ teaspoons cornflour
0	1 tablespoon cold water
28.5	**total grams carbohydrate**

Cut bitter melon crossways into 4-cm (1½-in) slices, discarding stem end and pointed tip. With a small, sharp knife remove spongy centre and seeds and discard, leaving short, tubular sections of melon.

Remove skin from fish. Chop fish very finely, discarding any bones. Shell, de-vein and chop prawns finely. Mix fish and prawns with salt, ginger, egg white and cornflour. Fill sections of melon with this mixture, rounding the filling slightly on one end of each section. Heat oil in a wok or frying pan and fry the melon, rounded end down, until fish is just starting to brown. Turn over and fry on other end. Use a frying spoon to lift pieces of melon onto a plate.

Sauce: Rinse salted beans in a strainer under cold water for a few seconds, then drain off liquid, put beans on a wooden board and mash well with a fork. Mix with crushed garlic. Fry this mixture in the oil remaining in wok, add sugar and stock or water and bring to the boil.

Return pieces of melon to pan, rounded end upwards, cover and simmer over very low heat for 20 minutes. Lift stuffed melon sections onto a serving plate. To mixture in pan add cornflour mixed with a little cold water and stir over medium heat until it thickens slightly. Pour over the melon pieces and serve with rice.

Stuffed Bitter Melon in Black Bean Sauce

Stir-Fried Onions and Celery

Serves: 2–4

9	1 medium onion
2	2 sticks celery
0	1 tablespoon peanut oil
Tr	½ teaspoon crushed garlic
Tr	½ teaspoon finely grated fresh ginger
2	1 tablespoon light soy sauce
2	¼ teaspoon sugar
0	½ teaspoon sesame oil
16	**total grams carbohydrate**

Peel onion, cut in 8 wedges lengthways and separate the layers. Cut celery into thin half-moon slices, angling the knife on a slant.

Heat a wok, add peanut oil and swirl to coat wok. Add garlic, ginger and vegetables all at once and stir-fry on high heat for 2 minutes. Sprinkle with soy sauce, sugar and sesame oil, toss and serve immediately.

Stir-Fried Lettuce

Serves: 2

12	1 small, firm iceberg lettuce
0	1 tablespoon peanut oil
Tr	½ teaspoon crushed garlic
0	¼ teaspoon salt
Tr	¼ teaspoon finely grated fresh ginger
1	2 teaspoons light soy sauce
0	1 teaspoon sesame oil
14	**total grams carbohydrate**

Lettuce cooked this way is usually a base on which to serve meat or seafood but you can serve it as a filling second dish to take the place of carbohydrates like rice or noodles. It also makes a delicious quick lunch.

Wash lettuce, drain and dry well. Cut into halves lengthways, then cut each half twice lengthways and twice crossways. This gives chunky, bite-sized pieces.

Heat a wok, add oil and swirl wok so oil coats inner surface. Add the garlic crushed with the salt and the ginger and stir quickly, then add the lettuce and toss on medium high heat for 30 seconds. Turn off heat. Add soy sauce and sesame oil, toss to distribute seasoning and serve at once. Lettuce should retain a crisp texture.

Bean Sprouts with Barbecued Pork   *Serves: 2–4*

20	500 g (1 lb) fresh bean sprouts
3	185 g (6 oz) barbecued pork fillet (see page 126)
0	2 tablespoons peanut oil
Tr	1 clove garlic, bruised
1	2 slices ginger
Tr	1 tablespoon dry sherry
2	1 tablespoon light soy sauce
0	1 teaspoon sesame oil
27	**total grams carbohydrate**

Wash the bean sprouts and pinch off any straggly tails. Shred the barbecued pork into pieces about the same size as the bean sprouts.

Heat a wok, add peanut oil and heat for half a minute, swirl wok to coat sides, add the garlic and ginger and fry until they are brown. Remove and discard. Add the pork to the flavoured oil and stir-fry for a few seconds, just until heated through. Add bean sprouts and toss over high heat for 1 minute, then add sherry, soy sauce, sesame oil and toss to distribute flavours. Serve at once.

Spinach with Dried Prawns   *Serves: 2–4*

1	16 dried prawns (shrimp)
13.5	1 large bunch spinach
0	2 tablespoons peanut oil
4	2 spring onions (scallions), finely chopped
2	½ teaspoon sugar
0	½ teaspoon salt
2	1 tablespoon oyster sauce
0	1 teaspoon sesame oil
22.5	**total grams carbohydrate**

Although some large dried prawns are available, for this recipe use the small variety. The freeze-dried ones that are light in colour are preferable, but if not readily available use the small sun-dried prawns.

Soak prawns in hot water for 20 minutes. Drain, reserving liquid. Wash spinach well, remove tough stems. Put leaves into a saucepan with just the water that clings to them. Steam for 8–10 minutes. Drain away any liquid and roughly chop the leaves.

Heat peanut oil in a wok, add the prawns and chopped spring onions and stir-fry for 1 minute. Add ¼ cup of the water the prawns soaked in, the sugar, salt, oyster sauce and sesame oil. Add the spinach and toss over medium high heat for 1 minute. Serve hot..

Steamboat, Stock and Soups

Soups are very filling and can be used at every meal. Have a quantity of stock ready in the freezer to form the basis for different soups and you will see that the actual putting together of the ingredients takes only a few minutes.

Steamboat

This is a great way to entertain, combining delicious low carbohydrate food and fun in a do-it-yourself meal. A selection of thinly sliced food is arranged on platters and each person cooks meat, seafood and vegetables in the bubbling stock, holding it in chopsticks or a wire basket and dipping it in the stock for a minute or even less.

The picturesque steamboat is a utensil for cooking at the table with a central chimney surrounded by a moat. It is heated by coals, which should be lit an hour or more before the meal in an outdoor barbecue or a metal bucket. This gives them a chance to be well alight and glowing.

Before starting the meal, pour some stock into the moat of the steamboat to prevent the vessel overheating when the coals are placed in it. Put the cover on the pot so that particles of coal cannot fall into the soup, then with tongs transfer the hot coals or briquettes to the chimney. Heat may be regulated by opening or closing the flue in the base of the steamboat. Place the utensil on a heavy metal tray covered with foil and place the tray on a thick wooden board. Steamboats made of brass or anodized metal are sold at oriental stores but if you don't have one use an electric wok or deep fryer three-quarters filled with stock. If some ingredients are not obtainable, substitute others with similar carbohydrate counts, for example, chicken instead of pork, mussels instead of scallops, broccoli instead of Chinese cabbage. The dipping sauces are served separately. Guests make a choice and put the sauce in the small sauce dish on their plate.

Steamboat Stock

0	1 kg (2 lb) chicken backs
0	12 cups cold water
0	1 whole star anise
1	6 slices fresh ginger
0	1 teaspoon whole black peppercorns
9	1 onion
0	salt to taste
10	**total grams carbohydrate**

Put all ingredients into a large pan, bring to the boil, skim surface. Cover and simmer gently until reduced to 8 cups. Strain stock before using.

Sauces for Dipping

Ginger-soy sauce: Mix together 2 teaspoons finely grated fresh ginger with ¼ cup soy sauce and ¼ cup water. 7 total grams carbohydrate.

Chilli-vinegar sauce: Combine ¼ cup soy sauce, ¼ cup water, 2 tablespoons vinegar and 2 teaspoons hot chilli sauce. 9 total grams carbohydrate.

Garlic-soy sauce: Crush 2 small cloves garlic with ½ teaspoon salt. Bring to the boil with ¼ cup soy sauce, 3 tablespoons dry sherry and 3 tablespoons water. Simmer 1 minute. 10 total grams carbohydrate.

Steamboat Dinner

Serves: 6

0	500 g (1 lb) fillet or rump steak
0	500 g (1 lb) lean pork fillet
8	500 g (1 lb) fresh raw prawns (shrimp)
8	250 g (8 oz) fresh or frozen scallops
12	125 g (4 oz) snow peas or sliced green beans
7.2	4 squares fresh bean curd
10	250 g (8 oz) fresh bean sprouts
8.4	375 g (12 oz) Chinese cabbage (gai choy or choy sum)
10	8–10 cups chicken stock (see page 156)

63.6   total grams carbohydrate

Trim beef of all fat and place in the freezer until partially frozen and firm enough to cut into paper-thin slices. Arrange on plate. Do the same with the pork fillet.

Shell and de-vein the prawns, thaw scallops if frozen and wash well, removing any sandy tracts.

String snow peas and leave whole if they are bite-sized. Cut squares of bean curd into thin slices. Wash bean sprouts and pinch off any straggly brown tails. Wash Chinese cabbage and cut stems into bite-sized pieces. Arrange ingredients on separate plates or two large platters.

Set each place with a plate, chopsticks, bowl, porcelain spoon and small sauce dish. Prepare steamboat, filling the moat three-quarters full with hot stock, place it on the table and let the stock come to the boil before removing the cover of the steamboat.

Guests select their food and hold it in the bubbling stock, from about 30 seconds for a slice of steak to 90 seconds or so for a medium-sized prawn.

When all the meats and seafood have been cooked and eaten, the vegetables are added to the broth, the lid replaced so that it simmers for a few minutes, then the soup is ladled into bowls to make a fitting finale to the meal.

Fish Stock

0	1.5 kg (3 lb) fish heads and trimmings
0	6 cups cold water
0	10 peppercorns
Tr	3 slices fresh ginger
5	1 carrot
2	2 stalks celery
9	1 large onion
Tr	2 stalks coriander
17	total grams carbohydrate

Wash fish trimmings thoroughly. Put into a large pan with cold water to cover, add remaining ingredients and bring to the boil. Cover and simmer 15 minutes. Strain stock and use in soups or as part of the liquid in seafood dishes.

Chicken Stock

0	chicken bones and trimmings (giblets, neck, feet, etc.)
0	6 cups cold water
0	10 peppercorns
2	2 small stalks celery with leaves
9	1 onion
1	3 or 4 coriander or parsley stalks
Tr	2 slices fresh ginger
0	salt to taste
12.5	total grams carbohydrate

Put bones and trimmings in a saucepan, add water and other ingredients, bring to the boil. Cover and simmer 45 minutes to 1 hour. Strain. Skim if necessary. The stock is now ready for use in soups and sauces. If stock is fatty, chill until fat congeals on surface, remove and discard.

Prawn Stock

0	heads and shells from 1 kg (2 lb) raw prawns (shrimp)
0	8 cups cold water
0	10 peppercorns
1	3 slices fresh ginger
5	1 carrot
2	2 stalks celery
9	1 large onion
Tr	2 stalks coriander (cilantro)
1	2 cloves garlic
18.5	**total grams carbohydrate**

Wash prawn heads and shells and drain very well, then wrap in paper towels and press out excess moisture. Heat 2 tablespoons oil in a saucepan and fry the prawn heads and shells on high heat, stirring. They will turn bright pink. Add the water and remaining ingredients and bring to the boil. Cover and simmer 30 minutes. Strain stock and use in soups or as part of the liquid in seafood dishes.

Pork Stock

0	1 kg (2 lb) pork bones
0	8 cups cold water
9	1 onion
2	1 stalk celery with leaves
0	1 star anise
Tr	4 coriander or parsley stalks (cilantro)
0	3 teaspoons salt
11.5	**total grams carbohydrate**

Put bones into a large pan with water to cover. Add all other ingredients. Bring to the boil, then cover and simmer for 2 hours. Strain and allow to cool, then chill. Remove fat from surface. Use as a base for soup or as part of the liquid in sauces for beef, chicken or pork dishes.

Combination Long Soup

2	4 dried Chinese mushrooms
Tr	2 eggs, beaten
0	salt and pepper to taste
0	few drops sesame oil
34	1 bundle fine egg noodles
12	6 cups chicken stock (see page 156) (or water and stock cubes)
0	125 g (4 oz) lean pork or chicken
0	1 tablespoon peanut oil
Tr	1 clove garlic, bruised
1	2 slices fresh ginger
4	2 cups shredded Chinese cabbage
5.2	½ cup diced canned bamboo shoot
4	2 tablespoons soy sauce
Tr	2 tablespoons Chinese wine or sherry
0	salt to taste
0	½ teaspoon sesame oil

63.7	**total grams carbohydrate**

Long soup and short soup take their names from the different kinds of noodles used in them. In long soup there are the long strands of fine egg noodles. In short soup there are little dumplings of meat and seafood mixture enclosed in a square of noodle dough. The low carbohydrate versions of these recipes have a much reduced quantity of noodles.

Soak dry mushrooms in hot water for 30 minutes, discard stems and slice mushrooms finely.

Season eggs with a little salt and pepper. Heat an omelette pan, grease lightly with a few drops of sesame oil, and pour in half the beaten egg to make a thin omelette. Repeat with remaining egg. Slice finely and set aside.

Cook noodles for 2 minutes in plenty of lightly salted boiling water. Drain in colander and run cold water through to separate. Drain again.

Heat chicken stock.. Shred pork or chicken very finely. Heat peanut oil in a wok, fry garlic and ginger and discard when they are brown. Add pork or chicken to the flavoured oil, fry quickly, stirring, until colour changes. Add vegetables, fry 2 minutes longer.

Add fried mixture and noodles to chicken stock, return to the boil. Add soy sauce, sherry and salt to taste. Stir in sesame oil. Serve immediately, garnished with strips cut from a plain omelette.

Combination Soup

0	250 g (8 oz) chicken, lean pork or beef
0	6 cups water
1	1 clove garlic
1	2 slices fresh ginger
1	1 stalk celery
0	2 teaspoons salt
2	125 g (4 oz) cooked prawns (shrimp)
6	3 cups Chinese cabbage, sliced
6	3 spring onions (scallions), cut in 5 cm (2 in) lengths
0	few drops sesame oil
17	total grams carbohydrate

Use any combination of meat and vegetables.

If using chicken, use wings or thighs for preference. Cut pork or beef into thin slices.

Place meat in a saucepan, add water, garlic, ginger, celery and salt and bring to the boil. Cover and simmer for 30 minutes. Remove ginger and garlic and discard.

If chicken thighs or other large joints are used, remove flesh from bones, cut into dice. Discard bones.

Add prawns and vegetables, return to the boil for 1 minute, stir in sesame oil and serve.

Soup with Vegetables

6	3 cups chicken stock (see page 150)
6	12 small sprigs of broccoli
6	60 g (2 oz) snow peas (mange-tout)
1	2 tablespoons finely chopped coriander (cilantro)
0	few drops sesame oil
19	total grams carbohydrate

Bring chicken stock to the boil. Add the broccoli and cook for about 2 minutes, add snow peas and cook for 2–3 minutes longer. Remove from heat, stir in coriander and sesame oil and serve at once.

Short Soup (Wonton Soup)

Serves: 4

1	60 g (2 oz) raw prawns (shrimp)
0	60 g (2 oz) minced (ground) pork
8	4 spring onions (scallions), chopped
2	1 tablespoon light soy sauce
Tr	1 clove garlic, crushed
Tr	¼ teaspoon finely grated fresh ginger
25	60 g (2 oz) wonton wrappers
8	4 cups chicken stock (see page 156)
0	few drops sesame oil
45	**total grams carbohydrate**

Shell and de-vein prawns and chop finely. Mix together prawns, pork, half the spring onions, soy sauce, garlic and ginger.

Place a small amount of the meat filling on each square of wonton pastry and fold in two diagonally, moistening edges and pressing together. Then bring the two base corners together so they overlap and use a dab of the filling mixture to hold them together.

Drop wontons into the boiling stock, return to the boil and cook for about 7 minutes. Turn off heat, add sesame oil, sprinkle with remaining spring onions and serve at once.

Egg Flower Soup

Serves: 4

10	4 cups chicken stock (see page 156)
Tr	2 tablespoons Chinese wine or dry sherry
0	1 teaspoon sesame oil
0	salt to taste
Tr	2 eggs
0	½ teaspoon salt
2	1 spring onion (scallion), finely sliced
13	**total grams carbohydrate**

This simple, nourishing soup can be made in a few minutes, using chicken stock cubes. The beaten egg will set when poured into the boiling soup and look like chrysanthemum petals. For a low cholesterol version, use egg whites instead of whole eggs.

Bring stock to the boil, add sherry and sesame oil. Taste and add salt if necessary. Season beaten eggs with ½ teaspoon salt, pour slowly into the boiling soup. Stir once or twice. Serve at once, sprinkled with sliced spring onion.

Short Soup (Wonton Soup)

Meatball and Cabbage Soup

0	250 g (8 oz) ground pork and veal
Tr	½ teaspoon finely grated fresh ginger
Tr	½ teaspoon finely grated garlic
2	1 tablespoon finely chopped spring onion (scallion)
1	2 teaspoons light soy sauce
0	¼ teaspoon salt
12	6 cups pork or chicken stock (see page 156)
6	3 cups finely shredded Chinese cabbage (wongah bak)
Tr	1 tablespoon dry sherry
0	½ teaspoon sesame oil
22.5	**total grams carbohydrate**

Once again, an adapted recipe that cuts down on the richness of the original and still tastes great. Pork and veal mince is substituted for pure pork, which is richer.

Combine ground meat with ginger, garlic, spring onion, soy sauce and salt. Mix thoroughly and with oiled hands form into small balls no larger than 2.5 cm (1 in) in diameter. Bring stock to the boil, drop in the balls and turn heat low. Cover and simmer for 5 minutes. Add shredded cabbage and return to the boil, cook uncovered for a further 8–10 minutes. Stir in sherry and sesame oil and serve.

Winter Melon Soup

0	1 chicken breast or 2 thighs
0	½ teaspoon salt
0	¼ teaspoon white pepper
Tr	1 small clove garlic, crushed
Tr	1 teaspoon dry sherry
Tr	1 teaspoon light soy sauce
2	4 dried Chinese mushrooms
12	500 g (1 lb) winter melon
12	6 cups chicken stock (see page 156)
27.5	total grams carbohydrate

A wonderfully non-fattening soup—the winter melon has no more calories or carbohydrates than a cucumber. In season, winter melon may be bought by weight at Chinese greengrocers or delicatessens.

Skin and bone the chicken and cut the flesh into small dice. Mix with the salt, pepper, garlic, sherry and soy sauce and set aside while preparing other ingredients.

Soak the dried mushrooms in hot water for 30 minutes, then discard stems and cut caps into thin slices. Peel the winter melon. Remove central fibres and seeds and discard, slice melon into thin slices and then cut into bite-sized squares.

Bring stock to the boil, add mushrooms and melon and simmer for 10 minutes, add chicken and simmer 5–8 minutes longer. Serve at once.

Crab and Egg Soup

Crab and Egg Soup

Serves: 4

2	1 mud crab or blue-swimmer crab or picked crab meat
8	4 cups chicken stock (see page 156)
1	2 eggs, slightly beaten
5	2 teaspoons cornflour (cornstarch)
0	2 tablespoons cold water
6	3 spring onions (scallions), finely sliced
22	**total grams carbohydrate**

If using fresh crab, cook in water for 10 minutes, cool, then pick out flesh and reserve. Discard shell and fibrous tissue from stomach. Flake crab meat, discarding any bony tissue.

Bring stock to the boil. Slowly dribble in the beaten eggs. Stir gently. After 2 minutes stir in the cornflour mixed smoothly with the cold water, return soup to the boil and stir constantly until it is clear and slightly thickened.

Add crab meat and heat through. Serve immediately, sprinkled with sliced spring onions.

Prawn Ball Soup

Serves: 4

PRAWN BALLS

8	500 g (1 lb) raw prawns (shrimp)
Tr	¼ teaspoon finely grated fresh ginger
0	½ teaspoon salt
Tr	1 egg yolk
2.5	1 teaspoon cornflour (cornstarch)

SOUP

8	4 cups fish or chicken stock (see page 156)
Tr	1 tablespoon Chinese wine or dry sherry
2.8	3 tablespoons canned bamboo shoot, sliced, optional
0	½ teaspoon sesame oil
4	2 spring onions (scallions), finely chopped
26.8	**total grams carbohydrate**

Shell and de-vein prawns and chop very finely. Combine with all other ingredients, form into balls 2.5 cm (1 in) in diameter and drop into simmering stock, return to simmering point, cook for about 3 minutes.

Stir in Chinese wine or dry sherry, bamboo shoot, sesame oil and finely chopped spring onions and serve hot.

Fish Ball Soup with Bamboo Shoots

Serves: 4

2	4 dried Chinese mushrooms
10	5 cups fish stock (see page 156)
10	16–20 small fish balls
1	1 tablespoon finely shredded fresh ginger
5.2	½ cup canned bamboo shoot, cut into matchstick strips
1	1 cup finely shredded Chinese cabbage
2	1 spring onion (scallion), cut in thin slices
0	salt to taste
0	½ teaspoon sesame oil

31.2   total grams carbohydrate

In Chinese delicatessens ready-cooked fish balls may be purchased for adding to soup and other mixed dishes. These have a certain amount of cornflour in them, so make allowance for this when adding up your carbohydrate total.

Soak dried mushrooms in hot water for 30 minutes, discard stems and slice caps finely. Bring stock to the boil, add all ingredients and simmer for 5 minutes or until cabbage is tender. Stir in sesame oil and serve hot.

Abalone and Mushroom Soup

Serves: 4

2	4–6 dried Chinese mushrooms
1.3	half of 1 x 250 g (8 oz) can abalone
0	125 g (4 oz) chicken or pork fillet
10	5 cups chicken stock
Tr	dash of light soy sauce
0	salt to taste
0	½ teaspoon sesame oil

13.8   total grams carbohydrate

Soak mushrooms in hot water for 20 minutes, discard stems and slice caps. Reserve liquid from can of abalone and cut 1 abalone into thin crosswise slices. Slice chicken or pork into very thin slices. Bring stock to the boil, add mushrooms and ½ cup of liquid from abalone, simmer 5 minutes. Add chicken or pork and cook until meat changes colour, then add the soy sauce and salt and the abalone. Do not boil, just heat through. Stir in sesame oil and serve.

Shark Fin Soup

2	6 dried Chinese mushrooms
0	1 chicken breast
20	8–10 cups strong chicken stock
1	1 can shark fin
2	1 tablespoon light soy sauce
1	¼ cup dry sherry
7.5	3 teaspoons cornflour (cornstarch)
0	2 tablespoons cold water
Tr	1 egg, slightly beaten
Tr	2 thin slices cooked ham cut into matchstick strips
34.5	total grams carbohydrate

For special occasions, when something really luxurious is called for, treat yourself to this banquet soup. One can of shark fin makes quite enough soup for 8–10 people, so it will be suitable for entertaining and you still won't be departing from your Chinese slimming diet. Using dried shark's fin makes this a dish that requires days of preparation, so I suggest using the canned product.

Soak the mushrooms in hot water for 20 minutes, discard stems and slice the caps very thinly, then cut the slices into fine strips. Skin and bone the chicken breast, slice as finely as possible.

Bring the stock to the boil with the shark fin, soy sauce and sherry. Add the mushrooms and chicken and when it returns to the boil stir in the cornflour mixed with water and keep on stirring until it boils and thickens slightly. Dribble in beaten egg and stir so it sets in fine shreds. Garnish soup with ham and serve at once.

Prawn Soup with Bean Starch Noodles

Serves: 4

8	500 g (1 lb) raw prawns (shrimp)
12	6 cups prawn stock (see page 157)
1	10 dried lily buds (golden needles)
2	5 dried Chinese mushrooms
17	½ cup soaked bean starch noodles (fenszu)
0	1 tablespoon peanut oil
Tr	1 teaspoon finely grated fresh ginger
Tr	½ teaspoon finely grated garlic
1	4 tablespoons finely chopped coriander (cilantro)
2	1 tablespoon light soy sauce
0	salt to taste
Tr	1 egg, slightly beaten
44.5	**total grams carbohydrate**

Shell and de-vein the prawns and if large cut in halves down the centre. While stock simmers soak the lily buds and dried mushrooms (separately) in hot water for 30 minutes. Discard the hard ends of the lily buds and tie each stem in a knot. Cut off stems of mushrooms and slice the caps finely. Soak a few strands of noodles in hot water for 10 minutes, drain and measure ½ cup. (It would not matter if slightly more noodles were used, but it would increase the carbohydrate content of the recipe as these noodles are made from mung bean starch.) Cut noodles into short lengths.

Heat the oil and fry the ginger and garlic over medium heat just until soft and starting to turn golden. Add the prawns and fry until they change colour, then add the stock, mushrooms, lily buds and noodles and bring to the boil. Simmer for 5 minutes, then stir in the coriander, soy sauce and salt. Dribble in the beaten egg and stir so it sets in little strands. Serve at once.

Prawn Soup with Bean Starch Noodles

Prawn and Mustard Cabbage Soup

Serves: 2

4	250 g (8 oz) raw prawns (shrimp)
0	1 tablespoon sesame oil
0	4 cups boiling water
0	1 teaspoon salt
2	1 cup Chinese mustard cabbage (gai choy), chopped
6	total grams carbohydrate

Shell prawns, reserving heads and shells. De-vein prawns and cut into halves or, if large, into quarters. Wash the heads and shells thoroughly, drain in a colander. Heat sesame oil in a saucepan, throw in the prawn heads and shells and fry over high heat, stirring until they turn pink. Add 4 cups boiling water, cover pan with lid and simmer for 20 minutes. Strain, discard heads and shells.

Make up prawn stock to 4 cups with water, return to saucepan and add salt to taste.

Chop cabbage into bite-sizedd pieces. Add prawns to soup, simmer for 5 minutes, then add cabbage. Simmer 2 minutes longer. Serve at once.

Note: Any variety of Chinese soup vegetables may be used in this soup, but if you ask for gai choy in a Chinese shop, you will be given the one I have used in this recipe. It looks like a small variety of Chinese mustard cabbage and has the same slightly pungent flavour.

Chicken Soup

Serves: 4–5

0	1 x 1 kg (2 lb) chicken
0	cold water
0	2 teaspoons salt
0	1 whole star anise
1	1 stalk celery, sliced
9	1 onion, sliced

GINGER-SOY SAUCE

Tr	1 teaspoon finely grated fresh ginger
6	¼ cup light soy sauce
0	2 tablespoons water
16.6	**total grams carbohydrate**

Skin chicken and put into a large saucepan with sufficient cold water to completely cover it. Add salt, star anise, celery and onion, bring to the boil, then simmer, covered, for 1 hour. If necessary, add more boiling water during cooking time.

Serve soup first, then serve chicken, which should be tender enough to break with chopsticks. Serve ginger-soy sauce with the chicken.

Ginger-soy sauce: Combine finely grated fresh ginger with light soy sauce and water.

Chicken and Cabbage Soup

Serves: 4

0	500 g (1 lb) chicken backs
0	1 star anise
Tr	2 slices fresh ginger
Tr	1 clove garlic, crushed
0	8 cups cold water
0	1 teaspoon salt
Tr	1 tablespoon Chinese wine or dry sherry
4	2 cups Chinese cabbage, finely sliced
5.5	**total grams carbohydrate**

Put chicken backs, star anise, ginger and garlic into a saucepan, add 8 cups water and bring to the boil. Cover and simmer for 1 hour.

Strain stock, add sherry and cabbage. Return to boil for 1 minute. Stir well and serve straight away.

Chicken and Asparagus Soup

Serves: 4

8	4 cups chicken stock (see page 156)
0	1 chicken breast
10	1 small can asparagus pieces or
	12 fresh asparagus tips
4	1½ teaspoons cornflour (cornstarch), optional
0	1 tablespoon cold water
Tr	1 tablespoon Chinese wine or sherry
Tr	2 eggs, beaten
23	total grams carbohydrate

Cut flesh from chicken breast into small dice. Set aside. Drain asparagus pieces, reserving liquid. Combine stock and canned asparagus or fresh spears cut into bite-sizedd pieces. Add diced chicken and bring to the boil. Lower heat, simmer 5 minutes, then add cornflour mixed with cold water and return to the boil, stirring until soup thickens slightly.

Add wine or sherry, slowly dribble in the beaten eggs, stirring. Add asparagus pieces, heat through and serve.

Chicken Soup with Cucumber Slices

Serves: 4

6	1 green cucumber
8	4 cups chicken stock (see page 156)
0	½ cup diced cooked chicken
1	2 tablespoons finely chopped coriander (cilantro)
0	½ teaspoon sesame oil
15	total grams carbohydrate

Peel the cucumber, cut in halves lengthways and scoop out the seeds. Cut into neat semi-circular slices. Bring the stock to the boil, add cucumber and cook for 8–10 minutes or until cucumber is tender but not mushy. Add chicken, coriander and sesame oil, stir well and serve.

Chicken and Bean Curd Soup

Serves: 4

2	4 dried Chinese mushrooms
2	1 tablespoon soy sauce
4	1 teaspoon sugar
0	1 small chicken breast
3.6	2 squares fresh bean curd
8	4 cups chicken stock (see page 156)
2	1 spring onion (scallion), finely sliced
0	¼ teaspoon sesame oil, optional
21.6	**total grams carbohydrate**

Soak mushrooms in hot water for 30 minutes, then cut off and discard stems, cut caps in thin slices and put into a small pan with ½ cup of the soaking water, the soy sauce and sugar. Bring to boil and cook until almost all liquid has evaporated.

Remove skin and bone from chicken breast and cut the meat into small dice. Cut bean curd squares into 3 strips, then across so that there are 9 equal-sized dice.

Bring chicken stock to the boil, add chicken and simmer for 1 minute. Add mushrooms and bean curd and return to simmering point. Add spring onion and sesame oil, turn off heat, cover and allow to stand for 1 minute, then serve.

Chicken Soup with Mustard Cabbage

Serves: 4

8	4 cups chicken stock (see page 156)
2	1 cup sliced gai choy (mustard cabbage)
1	1 tablespoon finely shredded fresh ginger
2	1 tablespoon finely sliced spring onion (scallion)
0	½ cup diced cooked chicken
Tr	1 tablespoon dry sherry
13.5	**total grams carbohydrate**

Bring the stock to the boil, add gai choy and ginger and simmer for 3 minutes. (The ginger should be cut into thin slices and then into thread-like strips.) Add the spring onion, chicken and sherry, stir and serve at once.

Chicken Velvet Soup with Straw Mushrooms

Serves: 4

0	1 chicken breast
0	3 tablespoons cold water
0	2 egg whites
0	¾ teaspoon salt
4	1 small can straw mushrooms or champignons
10	5 cups chicken stock (see page 156)
0	salt and pepper to taste
Tr	2 tablespoons finely chopped cooked ham
14.5	**total grams carbohydrate**

This diet version is not thickened with cornflour as the usual soup would be. If you have saved some carbohydrate grams from the rest of the day's allowance and want to splurge, thicken the stock by stirring in 3 or 4 level teaspoons cornflour mixed smoothly with 3 tablespoons cold water and letting it come to the boil so that it becomes clear. Then proceed as follows:

Skin and bone the chicken breast. Slice thinly, then with chopper (or two choppers if you can master the art of using two at once) chop the breast meat very finely. It should be reduced almost to a pulp. Gradually add the cold water and keep on chopping until the texture is light. Collect the chopped meat on the blade of the chopper and put it into a bowl. Beat the egg whites until frothy and fold into the chicken puree together with the salt. Drain mushrooms and cut each into halves lengthways.

Bring stock to the boil, add mushrooms and heat through. Taste and season with salt and pepper if necessary. Add mushrooms and return to simmering point, then add the chicken mixture and stir once. Cover pan and let it stand for 1 minute. Sprinkle chopped ham over soup and serve.

Chicken and Abalone Soup

Serves: 4

0	2 chicken thighs or 1 breast
0	½ teaspoon salt
0	pinch of white pepper
0	1 teaspoon peanut oil
2.5	1 teaspoon cornflour (cornstarch)
1.3	half can abalone
10	5 cups chicken stock (see page 156)
6	1 cup fresh bean sprouts
Tr	1 thin slice lean cooked ham, cut into fine shreds
0	½ teaspoon sesame oil

20.3	**total grams carbohydrate**

Remove skin and bones from chicken, slice meat finely. Mix with salt, pepper, peanut oil and cornflour and set aside. Drain abalone, reserving liquid from can. Slice abalone and cut slices into matchstick strips. Wash and drain bean sprouts and pinch off any straggly brown tails.

Bring stock to the boil with liquid from abalone, add chicken and stir until it returns to the boil. Add bean sprouts and simmer for 2 minutes. Add abalone strips and ham and stir just until heated through. Stir in sesame oil and serve.

Chicken and Abalone Soup

Soup with Chicken Livers

8	4 cups chicken stock (see page 156)
2	1 cup finely shredded Chinese cabbage
2	4 chicken livers
2	1 spring onion (scallion), sliced very finely
14	total grams carbohydrate

The chicken livers must be cooked just enough for them to lose their pinkness, but not over-cooked or they will become tough.

Bring the stock to the boil, add cabbage and simmer for 3 minutes. Add chicken livers and simmer for 8–10 minutes longer. Remove from heat, lift out chicken livers on slotted spoon and cut into thin slices. Sprinkle spring onion on soup, cover and leave for 1 minute, then serve.

Duck and Mushroom Soup

Serves: 4

2.5	8 dried Chinese mushrooms
0	bones from braised or roasted duck
0	8 cups water
0	1 whole star anise
1	2 slices ginger
4	2 spring onions (scallions)
1	few celery leaves
0	salt to taste
2	1 cup finely sliced Chinese cabbage
10.5	**total grams carbohydrate**

Soak mushrooms in hot water for 20 minutes, discard stems and cut caps into quarters. Put the duck bones and mushrooms into a saucepan with the water, star anise, ginger, spring onions and celery leaves. Bring to the boil, then turn heat low, cover and simmer for 1 hour.

Strain the stock, add salt to taste. Return mushrooms to strained stock, bring to the boil again, add the shredded cabbage and cook for 5 minutes or until cabbage is just tender. Serve hot.

Duck Soup with Bean Curd

Serves: 4

0	bones from cooked duck
0	8 cups water
0	1 whole star anise
1	2 slices ginger
9	1 medium onion
1	few celery leaves
3.6	2 squares fresh bean curd
2	1 spring onion (scallion), finely sliced
Tr	few leaves coriander (cilantro)
17.1	**total grams carbohydrate**

Simmer the duck bones with the water, star anise, ginger, onion and celery leaves for 1 hour in a saucepan. Strain and make up stock to 4 cups with hot water if necessary. Cut bean curd into small dice and add to the soup to heat through. Sprinkle with spring onion and coriander and serve hot.

Rice
and Noodles

Rice and noodles may form a substantial part of any other Chinese cookbook, but not this one. As explained in the Introduction, they contain approximately 18 grams of carbohydrate in each half-cup serving, so they should not be a dominant part of the diet.

White Rice

1½ cups water
1 cup short grain white rice

This will yield about 3 cups of cooked rice. Use your allowance the first day, then refrigerate the rice and reheat measured amounts as required to save you cooking rice each time you need it—and you don't have to eat rice every day, it keeps under refrigeration for up to one week. Remember that a ½ cup portion of cooked rice has a carbohydrate count of 18 grams

Wash rice in one or two changes of cold water and drain in a colander. Bring water to the boil, add rice and stir once. Return to the boil, then turn heat very low, cover pan tightly and cook without lifting lid for 15 minutes. Rice will stay hot in the covered pan for 30 minutes or longer.

If using stainless steel saucepan of the 'waterless' cooking type, which forms a seal between pan and lid, reduce cooking time to 10 minutes but leave the pan covered for a further 10 minutes before serving.

Golden Rice

½ cup natural brown rice
½ cup short grain white rice
2 cups water

This is a mixture of equal parts of natural brown (unpolished) rice and white rice. It is delicious, chewy, more nutritious and stays with you longer than white rice, so is ideal for this diet. It still contains 18 grams of carbohydrate per half-cup portion, so don't go overboard with quantities. Since unpolished rice takes longer to cook than white rice, the trick is to soak it for at least 2 hours before cooking.

Wash and soak the natural rice for at least 2 hours, then drain. Put it into a saucepan with the white rice and water, bring to the boil, then lower heat, cover tightly and cook for 25–30 minutes without lifting lid.

Simple Fried Rice

36	1 cup cold cooked rice
2	4 dried Chinese mushrooms
4	2 spring onions (scallions)
0	2 tablespoons peanut oil
0	1 teaspoon sesame oil
Tr	½ teaspoon finely grated fresh ginger
Tr	1 clove garlic, crushed
2	1 tablespoon soy sauce
0	salt to taste
45	**total grams carbohydrate**

The trick to making good fried rice is to cook the rice the day before or some hours ahead and allow it to cool completely. With wet fingers, separate grains and spread out on a tray. Refrigerate if time permits—this gives a firm texture to the fried rice.

Soak mushrooms in hot water for 30 minutes, then squeeze out as much liquid as possible. With a sharp knife cut off and discard stems, cut mushroom caps into thin slices. Finely chop the spring onions, green leaves and all.

Heat a wok, add both kinds of oil and fry the ginger and garlic, stirring, until golden. Add mushrooms and fry for a minute longer, then add rice and stir-fry until it is heated through. Add the spring onions and soy sauce and toss to combine thoroughly. Taste and add salt as required.

Remove from heat and serve at once.

Boiled Noodles

small bundle egg noodles
1 teaspoon peanut oil

Though noodles are a carbohydrate food and should be off-limits, some Chinese dishes positively cry out for them. You can have a small amount of noodles to off-set a salty sauce, but do remember that a ½ cup portion of cooked noodles has a carbohydrate count of almost 18 grams, so allow for that on your balance sheet. A small bundle of dry noodles will yield approximately 1 cup of cooked noodles, which has a carbohydrate value of 34.8 grams.

Soak noodles in hot water for about 10 minutes. The strands will separate and enable the noodles to cook evenly. Meanwhile, bring a large saucepan of water to the boil and add a teaspoon of peanut oil. Drain the soaked noodles and drop them into the boiling water. When water returns to the boil, cook fine noodles for 2–3 minutes, wide noodles for 3–4 minutes. Do not over-cook. Like properly cooked spaghetti, noodles should be tender but still firm to the bite.

At the end of cooking time drain noodles in a large colander. If not serving immediately, run cold water through the noodles to rinse off excess starch and cool the noodles so they don't continue to cook in their own heat. Drain thoroughly and serve with stir-fried dishes or use in soups and braised noodle dishes.

Glossary

Bamboo shoot: Sold in cans either water-packed or braised. Unless otherwise stated, the recipes in this book call for the water-packed variety. After opening can, store in a bowl of fresh water in the refrigerator, replacing water daily, for up to 10 days. Winter bamboo shoots are preferable, being more tender. Cans are usually labelled.

Bean sauces: There are many kinds of bean sauce: salty, sweet and hot. The most basic are mor sze jeung (ground bean sauce), smooth and thick, and min sze jeung, a thick paste of mashed and whole fermented soy beans. The most popular sweet bean sauce is hoi sin jeung (see separate entry). The hot bean sauces (mostly used in Sichuan style dishes) are chilli bean sauce, hot bean sauce and soy chilli sauce. Some are oily, some are not. All these bean sauces are too thick to pour. Use the one specified in the recipe for the best results. They will keep without refrigeration.

Bean sprouts: Green mung beans are used for bean sprouts. They are sold fresh in Chinese stores and most supermarkets and health food stores. The canned variety are not recommended. Substitute thinly sliced celery for crunchy texture, though flavour is different. Fresh bean sprouts may be stored in refrigerator for a week in plastic bag, or cover with water and change water daily.

Chilli sauce: Chinese chilli sauce is different to other chilli sauce. Substitute Tabasco or other hot pepper sauce, not one of the sweet chilli sauces. Keeps indefinitely.

Chinese mushrooms: (doong gwoo) These dried mushrooms are sold by weight. They are expensive but add incomparable flavour. Do not substitute fresh mushrooms or dried continental mushrooms. Soak in hot water for 30 minutes before cooking. Stems and soaking water may be saved for flavouring stock. If you enjoy the flavour, a time-saving tip is to soak and cook more than you need for one recipe, and keep the rest refrigerated and ready to add to other recipes.

Chinese parsley: More correctly known as fresh coriander or cilantro. This dark green pungent herb is widely used in Chinese cooking. Do not use more than the amount stated as it is likely to overpower other flavours. Store in tightly closed plastic bags in refrigerator for two weeks.

Chinese sausages (lap cheong): Dried sausages filled only with spiced lean and fat pork, which will keep without refrigeration. Steam for 10 minutes until soft and plump, cut into thin slices to serve or include in dishes.

Five spice powder: A combination of ground anise, fennel, cinnamon, cloves and Sichuan pepper, it gives distinctive flavour in cooking and is also used as a dip, combined with salt.

Garlic: Use fresh garlic in Chinese food, dried garlic flakes or powder are too pungent. In some instances the garlic clove is fried in the oil, then lifted out and discarded, leaving just a delicate flavour.

Ginger root: A basic seasoning in Chinese food. Buy fresh root ginger from Chinese food shops, greengrocers, supermarkets. Store by freezing in a plastic bag, peeling and bottling in a jar of dry sherry (store in refrigerator); or burying in moist soil and watering frequently. Dig up a piece as needed, replace remaining ginger root in soil and keep moist. If you are able to buy it frequently, store in the crisper section of the refrigerator where it will keep fresh for about three weeks. Ginger is also available sliced in cans and this is the best substitute for fresh ginger. Do not use powdered ginger as a substitute.

Hoi sin sauce: A sweet, spicy, reddish brown sauce of thick pouring consistency made from soy beans, garlic, spices. Used in barbecued pork dishes and as a dip. Keep in well covered jar. Keeps indefinitely.

Lily buds: Also known as 'golden needles' or lotus buds though they are not lotus but day lilies (Hemerocallis), these dried golden buds, long and narrow, have a very delicate flavour and are said to be very nutritious. Soak for half an hour or longer in hot water. Cut in half crossways or tie in a knot for easier eating.

Lotus root: Sometimes available fresh or frozen. Peel, cut into slices and use as directed. Dried lotus root must be soaked for at least 20 minutes in hot water with a little lemon juice added to preserve whiteness. Canned lotus root is readily available and may be stored in the refrigerator for a few days once opened.

Mushrooms, Chinese dried: See Chinese mushrooms.

Oyster sauce: Adds delicate flavour to all kinds of dishes. Made from oysters cooked in soy sauce and brine, this thick brown sauce keeps indefinitely once opened.

Red bean curd: A salty, pungent, seasoning used in small quantities.

Red bean paste: A thick, sweet paste made from red soy beans and used in barbecue type dishes.

Salted black beans: Made from soy beans, heavily salted and preserved in cans. Similar to salted yellow beans. Rinse before using to prevent oversalting in recipes. Substitute extra soy sauce. Store in covered container in refrigerator after opening for six months or longer, adding a little peanut oil if top dries out.

Sesame oil: This oil is extracted from toasted sesame seeds, giving it a rich amber colour and totally different flavour from the lighter sesame oil sometimes sold in health stores. For the recipes in this book. purchase sesame oil from Chinese stores. Use in small quantities for flavouring, not as a cooking medium.

Snow peas: Also known as mange-tout or sugar peas. Sold fresh in season, these are mainly a speciality of Chinese market gardeners but large seed companies now sell the seeds in packets under the name of sugar peas. They are never cooked for longer than a minute or two and are eaten pod and all. The French name for them is mange-tout. They are sometimes available frozen, but lack the delightful crispness of the fresh peas. Store fresh snow peas for a few days in a plastic bag or in a bowl of water in the refrigerator. String them before using.

Soy sauce: Indispensable in Chinese cooking, this versatile sauce enhances the flavour of every basic ingredient in a dish. Different grades are available. Dark soy sauce is used in most instances, but light soy is used when cooking chicken or seafood, or in soups where the delicate flavour and colour of the dish must be preserved. Keeps indefinitely.

Spring onion: The member of the onion family known as a shallot in Australia or scallion in the US, is correctly called a spring onion or green onion almost everywhere else. Use the straight, slender onions without large, well developed bulbs.

Spring roll wrappers: Thin, white sheets of pastry sold in plastic packets. Usually frozen. Unused wrappers may be refrozen. Large wonton wrappers may not be substituted.

Star anise: One of the prettiest seed pods, it looks like a reddish brown, eight-petalled flower. Used in stocks or master sauces for red-cooked dishes, it imparts a licorice flavour.

Straw mushrooms: Unlike dried mushrooms with their strong flavour, these mushrooms are as delicately flavoured as champignons. They are shrouded in their own little 'tent' that envelopes the stalk and cap with a thin skin. Sold in cans.

Walnuts: Peeled walnuts are sold by weight in Chinese grocery stores and are perfect for using in fried dishes, as the thin skin which turns bitter through cooking has been removed. If peeled walnuts are not available, use the canned, salted walnuts also sold in Chinese stores. These do not need further cooking.

Water chestnuts: Sometimes available fresh, the brownish-black skin must be peeled away with a sharp knife, leaving the crisp, slightly sweet kernel. Available in cans, already peeled. After opening, store in water in refrigerator for a week or 10 days, changing water daily.

Wonton wrappers: Small squares of fresh noodle dough bought from Chinese stores. Refrigerate, well wrapped in plastic, for a week.

Wood fungus: Sold by weight, wood fungus in its dry state looks like greyish black pieces of paper. Soaked in hot water for 10 minutes it swells to translucent brown shapes like curved clouds or a rather prettily shaped ear. It is sometimes known as 'cloud ear' fungus. Adds no flavour but has a distinctive, crunchy texture. Keeps indefinitely. In Chinese herbal medicine, it is prescribed to increase the fluidity of the blood and improve circulation.

Carbohydrate Values of Western Foods

While western foods may have no place in your actual Chinese diet, it is useful to know what the carbohydrate values of common foods are. You will be surprised, no doubt, to see that cream and butter and cheese won't deliver as many grams of carbohydrate or upset this eating plan as much as a couple of sweet biscuits. Read over the tables and be surprised. Remember the facts and use them.

You may not feel like Chinese food at breakfast time, or might not have time to whip up an oriental dish. Your tummy tells you it's time for a small bowl of oatmeal or cornflakes and the kitchen clock tells you it's all you have time for. Don't stress, just have your familiar breakfast. Make a note of the grams of carbohydrate in the portion. It will average about 12 grams of carbs in a half cup portion. Sugar adds 4 grams in each teaspoon. In a daily allowance of 80 grams, this isn't going to break the bank, so to speak. Oatmeal in particular, being a low glycaemic, high fibre food, will keep you feeling satisfied for a few hours. Watch what you eat at other meals and you need not step over your daily limit. Knowledge is power!

While enjoying Chinese food will keep you looking forward to main meals, there are always those other, in-between times, when something is called for but time does not permit you to create a Chinese banquet. That is the reason this table of carbohydrate values of western foods in included, so you can choose slices of cold meat or ham over a banana or a sandwich and not blow your carb allowance for the day.

Carbohydrate Values of Western Foods

	QUANTITY	CARBOHYDRATE (grams)
BISCUITS		
chocolate coated, plain	2 biscuits	15.0
cream filled, assorted	1	12.8
plain, sweet	2	12.3
Salada (Saltine)	3	8 8
Sao	2	12 5
shredded wheatmeal	1	6.2
Ryvita	1	7.5
Vita Wheat	1	4.2
BREAD		
brown	1 slice	12.3
raisin	1	13.5
rye		
dark	1	15.6
light	1	10.8
white	1	11.5
starch reduced	1	8.5
wholemeal	1	15.0
BUTTER		
	1 teaspoon	Tr (0.5)
	1 tablespoon	0.1
	250 g (½ lb)	1.6
CEREALS		
Cornflakes	½ cup	11.8
oatmeal, cooked	½ cup	11.7
Rice Bubbles (Krispies)	½ cup	11.7
wheatflake biscuit	1 biscuit	12 2
CHEESE		
cheddar	20 g (¾ oz)	.0
cottage, creamed	1 tablespoon	0.6
cream cheese	1 tablespoon	0.6
grated	1 tablespoon	.0
processed spread	1 tablespoon	0.2

	QUANTITY	CARBOHYDRATE (grams)
CREAM		
1 tablespoon	0.6	
½ cup	3.6	
FISH		
baked or steamed	2 small fillets	.0
crumbed and fried	1 fillet	11.6
fried in batter	1 fillet	14.3
FLOUR		
	1 tablespoon	7.4
	½ cup	41.4
FRUIT, DRIED		
currants	1 tablespoon	8.0
dates		
prunes		
raisins	1 tablespoon	9.7
sultanas	1 tablespoon	9.9
FRUIT, FRESH		
apple	1 small	13.8
apricot	3 medium	11.4
banana	1 medium	22 5
grapefruit	half	11.0
grapes	20 to 22	16 8
mandarines	1 large	11 2
oranges	1 medium	14.4
passionfruit	1 medium	6.3
peaches	1 medium	11.7
pear	1 medium	21.7
pineapple	1 slice 1 cm (½ in) thick	10.8
strawberries	12–14 medium	18.6
tomato	1 medium	4.5

Carbohydrate Values of Western Foods (continued)

	QUANTITY	CARBOHYDRATE (grams)
JUICES		
(canned and sweetened)		
apple	½ cup	13.8
grape	½ cup	19.9
grapefruit	½ cup	15.3
orange	½ cup	14.6
pineapple	½ cup	15.8
tomato	½ cup	4.9
MEATS		
Bacon		
fried	21 g (¾ oz)	0.4
grilled	15 g (½ oz)	0.4
raw	40 g (1½ oz)	0.4
Beef		
fillet, lean, grilled	2 average-size	.0
hamburger, with cereal	75 g (2½ oz)	11.9
roast, topside, lean	75 g (2½ oz)	.0
sausage, thick, grilled	110 g (3¾ oz)	10.5
T-bone, lean, grilled	1 average-size	.0
Chicken		
breast, boiled	110 g (3¾ oz)	.0
fried	135 g (4¾ oz)	3.9
Lamb		
chop, lean, grilled	110 g (3¾ oz)	.0
leg, roasted	2 thick slices	.0
Pork		
chop, grilled	80 g (2¾ oz)	.0
leg, roasted	75 g (2 ½ oz)	.0
Sausage		
devon	50 g (1¾ oz)	1.9
frankfurter, boiled	100 g (3¾ oz)	2.0

	QUANTITY	CARBOHYDRATE (grams)
Veal		
cutlet, crumbed, fried	140 g (5 oz)	12.1
grilled	100 g (3½ oz)	.0
rump, roasted	75 g (2½ oz)	.0
MILK		
condensed	1 tablespoon	14.7
evaporated	1 tablespoon	2.2
fresh	1 tablespoon	0.9
	½ cup	5.2
	2½ cups (1 pint imp.)	26.2
Full cream, dried	1 tablespoon	3.3
	1 cup	35.8
skim, dried	1 tablespoon	5.5
	1 cup	56.2
skimmed	1 tablespoon	1.0
	1 cup	11.0
PEANUTS		
	43 g (1½ oz)	8.3
VEGETABLES		
beans, boiled	½ cup	4.0
beetroot, canned	30 g (1 oz)	2.3
carrot, raw	60 g (2 oz)	5.1
cauliflower, boiled	60 g (2 oz)	2.5
Potato		
baked	90 g (3 oz)	19.7
boiled	90 g (3 oz)	17.1
crisps	22 g (¾oz)	11.0
French fries	90 g (3 oz)	29.3
mashed	20 g (¾ oz)	2.6
pumpkin, boiled	60 g (2 oz)	4.2
spinach, boiled	60 g (2 oz)	2.4
YOGHURT		
flavoured, with fruit	230 g (8 oz) carton	25.0
plain	230 g (8 oz) carton	13.1
skim	230 g (8 oz) carton	15.8

Carbohydrate Values of Chinese Foods

	QUANTITY	CARBOHYDRATE (grams)
A		
abalone	1 medium-size 100 g (3 ½ oz)	2.3
almonds	12 to 15	5
asparagus		
fresh/canned	6 to 7 spears	4
B		
bamboo shoot	½ cup 100 g (3½ oz)	5.2
bean sprouts, raw	½ cup	3
	125 g (4 oz)	5
bean curd, fresh	125 g (4 oz) (approx. 50 g (2 oz) per square)	3.6
bean sauce, chilli,		
chilli soy and other thick, unsweetened sauces	1 teaspoon	1
beans, green, boiled	½ cup	4
raw, sliced	100 g (3½ oz)	6
beef, various cuts,		
lean and fat	125 g (4 oz)	.0
beef stock	1 cup	2.5
bream	125 g (4 oz)	.0
broccoli, cooked	⅔ cup	5
raw	1 cup	5
Chinese	125 g (4 oz)	6.8
Brussels sprouts,		
cooked	½ cup = 5-6 sprouts	4.6
black beans,		
canned, salted	1 tablespoon	1
C		
cabbage, Chinese	125 g (4 oz)	3
capsicum, sliced or diced	½ cup	2
carrots, raw	1 small	5.1
cooked, drained	½ cup	5
cashew nuts	¼ cup	9
cauliflower, raw	50 g, ½ cup	3
	125 g (4 oz)	9.5

	QUANTITY	CARBOHYDRATE (grams)
celery, raw, diced	½ cup	2
chicken, raw or cooked	125 g (4 oz)	.0
liver, cooked	125 g (4 oz)	3.5
stock	1 cup	2.5
chilli sauce, sweet, barbecue, plum, other thick, sweet sauces	1 teaspoon	2
chillies, hot	1 medium-size	0.8
Chinese chilli sauce, unsweetened	1 teaspoon	0.5
Chinese sausage (lap cheong)	1 pair	2
coriander, fresh	1 tablespoon	0.5
cornflour	1 teaspoon	0.7
crab meat, flaked	500 g (1 lb)	5.4
crayfish, (spiny lobster)	1 medium-size	6
meat only	2 cm (1 in) piece	1
cucumber	100 g (3½ oz)	3 4
D		
Duck	125 g (4 oz)	.0
E		
eggplant	125 g (4 oz)	5
eggs		
whole	1 medium-size	0.3
white only	1 medium-size	0.2
yolk only	1 medium-size	0.1
F		
Fish		.0
G		
garlic	1 clove	0.5
ginger root, grated	1 teaspoon	0.5
H		
ham	60 g (2 oz)	0.5
hoi sin sauce	1 teaspoon	2
honey	1 teaspoon	6

Carbohydrate Values of Chinese Foods (continued)

	QUANTITY	CARBOHYDRATE (grams)
K		
kidneys		
beef	125 g (4 oz)	1
pork	125 g (4 oz)	1
L		
lamb		
lap cheong (Chinese sausage	1 pair	2
leeks	125 g (4 oz)	12.5
lemon juice	½ cup	8
lemons	1 medium-size	8
lettuce	1 small head	12
	2 small leaves	0.6
lily buds	10	3
lychee, fresh	125 g (4 oz)	20.5
lobster		
whole	500 g (1 lb)	0.6
meat only	500 g (1 lb)	2.3
lotus root	125 g (4 oz)	14
M		
master sauce	1 cup	18
mushrooms, raw	6 small	2
canned, not drained	½ cup	2
mustard cabbage greens	125 g (4 oz)	5
N		
noodles, cooked	½ cup	17.4
	1 cup	34.8
O		
oil, cooking or salad	1 tablespoon	0
onions, raw	1 medium	9
onions, spring	1 medium	2
oranges	1 medium	14.4
oyster sauce	1 tablespoon	2
P		
peas, green, cooked, fresh or frozen	½ cup	11.4

	QUANTITY	CARBOHYDRATE (grams)
pineapple, fresh, diced	½ cup	9.4
pork, roasted	125 g (4 oz)	0
prawns (shrimp), raw, shelled	125 g (4 oz)	2
R		
radishes, red and white	4 small	1
rice, white or brown (cooked)	½ cup	18
S		
sauce, oyster	1 tablespoon	2
scallops, cooked	6 medium-size	0
raw	125 g (4 oz)	4
sesame seeds, whole	125 g (4 oz)	22.6
	1 tablespoon	3
sherry, dry	3 tablespoons (2 oz)	1
silver beet, leaves only	1 bunch	13.5
boiled	½ cup	4.5
snow peas	125 g (4 oz)	12
soy sauce	1 tablespoon	2
soybean sprouts	125 g (4 oz)	6.6
spinach, boiled	½ cup	3.6
spring onions (scallions)	1 medium	2
squid	125 g (4 oz)	2
stock	1 cup	2
strawberries, raw	12 to 14 medium-size	8.6
sugar, white	1 teaspoon	4
brown	1 teaspoon	5
sweet chilli sauce	1 tablespoon	6
T		
tomato sauce	1 tablespoon	5.1
V		
vinegar	2 tablespoons	1
W		
walnuts, chopped	1 tablespoon	1
halves	½ cup	8
water chestnut, canned	8 chestnuts	19
chopped	1 tablespoon	3.5
wood fungus	2 tablespoons	0.5

Equivalent Terms

Most culinary terms in the English-speaking world can cross national borders without creating havoc in the kitchen. Nevertheless, local usage can produce some problems. The following list contains names of ingredients, equipment and cookery terms that are used in this book, but which may not be familiar to all readers.

USED IN THIS BOOK	ALSO KNOWN AS	USED IN THIS BOOK	ALSO KNOWN AS
absorbent paper	paper towels	okra	gumbo, ladies' fingers
almond essence	almond extract	papaw, pawpaw	papaya
belly pork	fresh pork side	pinch (of salt)	dash
boiling chicken/fowl	stewing chicken	plain flour	all-purpose flour
bream	sole	pork fat	fat back
capsicums	sweet or bell peppers	prawns	shrimp
celery stick	celery rib	rasher (of bacon)	slice
chuck steak	round steak, stewing steak	rockmelon	cantaloupe
chump (lamb)	leg steak	rump steak	sirloin
cornflour	cornstarch	Scotch fillet	sirloin
cutlets	chops	self-raising flour	self-rising flour
desiccated coconut	shredded coconut	(to) shell	(to) shuck, hull
essence	extract	shin (of meat)	shank
eggplant	eggplant, aubergine	sieve	strain / strainer
fillet (of meat)	tenderloin	(to) sift	(to) strain
frying pan	skillet	skirt steak	flank steak
gravy beef	stew beef	snapper, schnapper	sea bass
greaseproof paper	wax paper	snow peas	sugar peas, mange-tout
green prawns	raw shrimp	spring onions	scallions, green onions
grill/griller	broil/broiler	stock cubes	bouillon cubes
ground rice	rice flour	stone, seed, pip	pit
hard-boiled egg	hard-cooked egg	sultanas	seedless raisins
jewfish	halibut	tailor	blue fish, snapping mackerel
John Dory	Porgy, scup	tea towel	dish towel, glass cloth
king prawns	jumbo shrimp, scampi	vanilla pod	vanilla bean
kitchen paper	paper towels	(to) whisk	(to) whip, beat
mince/minced (meat)	ground		

Index

Index

Index